EXPAT

THE EASY WAY

Live and work successfully wherever you are

MARINDA SEISENBERGER

Expat the Easy Way

First published in 2015 by

Panoma Press Ltd

48 St Vincent Drive, St Albans, Herts, AL1 5SJ, UK

info@panomapress.com

www.panomapress.com

Book layout by Neil Coe.

Printed on acid-free paper from managed forests.

ISBN 978-1-909623-94-1

DEDICATION

I dedicate this book to all the members of my wonderful family who are spread around the globe – my precious parents in South Africa, my very special sister in Hong Kong, my big brother and his family in New Zealand and my darling niece in Ireland. We all know that the world is just a village.

Contents

Introduction

I shall never forget the comments from so many friends and acquaintances in early 1999 when I announced that I was emigrating from South Africa to Germany. "Germany? Why there? Why don't you go somewhere where they at least speak English? The Germans are so cold and they've got ZERO sense of humour! And they're bureaucratic and inflexible! Well, rather you than me! All the best to you then with the 'Sauer Krauts'!" I was stunned and when I finally did say anything, it was simply, "have any of you been there?" "No, thank goodness, but everybody knows the Germans!"

It was then that I started thinking about what people think of other nations and why. I also wondered how I would survive in the land of those that had just been described to me. One thing was sure, my interest in all things intercultural and international was ignited and this flame is fed by my daily encounters in a world of international communication culture.

Sixteen years later, I am still in Germany – happy on a multitude of levels and Germany has become my home of choice and a country that I love living and working in. I have met, worked with and become friends with countless expats, foreign tourists, Germans of mixed cultural descent and German "born-and-breds". My discussions, my interactions, my exchange of experiences, my work, my coaching and training sessions, my very own lessons learned, my laughter and tears, the stories that I have told and been told and my wonderful friendships with all these people, are what inspired me to write this book.

International relocation is a serious step. Lack of preparation and little awareness of what to expect can make it daunting and even dangerous. This book looks at the key dos and don'ts of living and working abroad. Learning the local lingo is a good start, but getting to grips with the nitty-gritty that constitutes daily life is vital for happiness and success. Whether you're going abroad for your company, for the love of your life, to study, to set up a new business yourself, to simply start a new life elsewhere, or for a gap year – this is your guide to getting it right.

Expat the Easy Way* – *live and work successfully wherever you are is my gift to all those who relocate internationally. It's a combination of my experiences, acquired knowledge and my thoughts and opinions on how best to cope with, and make the best of, this life-changing decision.

CHAPTER 1
AN EXPATRIATE

1.1 The term defined

The term "expatriate" derives from the Latin prefix ex (out of) and the noun patria (home country, native country, or fatherland). In today's globalised world, as the reasons for going abroad become more diverse, it's no longer easy to find a concrete definition for this term. The word "expat" is generally used, though, to refer to people who temporarily or permanently stay in a foreign country for a certain period of time, and plan to return to their home country eventually, although there are some who never return to their country of citizenship. Expats usually choose to leave their native country for a career boost or to fulfil a personal dream or goal, rather than as a result of economic and political trauma and necessity.

In this book, the term "expat" refers to individuals who establish their residence in the territory of another country for a temporary period that is, or is expected to be, of at least 12 months and a maximum of five years, having previously been resident in another country.

1.1.2 Types of expatriate

The individual situations of expats vary greatly and bring with them individual issues, but there seem to be a few common traits that are shared by many expats. They often have tertiary education and many expats have higher than average incomes. For many, their already good incomes are further supplemented by special allowances – these range from regular flights home to private tuition and schooling for their children. Relocation costs are usually paid by their companies and expat homes are often of a higher standard than those in their home countries. Expats going abroad without company support, for example to study or simply take a gap year and live and work somewhere else, also have a degree of financial security – at least to get them through the initial stages of the expat experience.

- ***The everyday expat***

The *everyday expat* is usually an employee sent abroad by their company or government.

Janine is one of these *everyday expats*. She works as a planning specialist for a global textile company in South Africa. In 2013 her company decided to send her to Hong Kong on a two-year assignment. Janine now lives in Kowloon and works for the Hong Kong branch office. "Having international experience is all the rage now and it really adds value to your CV – especially on the African continent," she says. After her assignment in Hong Kong, Janine will probably return to the same company in South Africa, but does not exclude going elsewhere for the same company.

Everyday expats usually stay in one place abroad from anywhere between a few months and a few years. They often return to their home bases at the end of such assignments, but some employees become so-called "serial expats" and either before returning home or soon after their return, are ready to take on another expat assignment – often for the same company, but also for new companies that attach a lot of value to their international work experience.

• *The grass is greener expat*

When his second child was born sixteen years after his first, Neil decided to leave his home country for a place he considered safer for his child to grow up in. He also believed that his child would have a more secure economic and employment future in New Zealand, so he and his wife and young son left for their country of choice and will never return to the country of their birth.

Grass is greener expats are usually disillusioned with life, or parts of it, in their own countries. This can range from high unemployment and very low salaries to crime and political instability. *Grass is greener* expats often stay on permanently in the countries they go to.

• *The home is where the heart is expat*

Adam has a particularly close relationship with his brother, Jonathan. When Jonathan relocated from England to Germany for work, it wasn't long before Adam decided to join him there. Mike and Angela relocated to Australia after their only daughter moved there for work and decided to stay. Leigh-Anne relocated from England to Ireland to join her boyfriend, George. Mika gave up her own job to join her husband in Istanbul for a three-year international assignment.

Home is where the heart is expats often stay on in the countries they move to and take on new or secondary citizenships to facilitate access to a host of official rights and benefits.

• *The global nomad expat*

Jörn is Swedish, but has spent nearly all of his adult life working abroad. As a self-employed IT consultant, he chooses projects of medium length (about 18 months each) with various companies and then moves to the relevant country. Jörn sees as home whichever country he is working in. An eternal nomad, he simply doesn't want to stay in one place for a long time and loves the exposure to international culture and business that he experiences with his work and lifestyle.

Global nomad expats travel extensively and continuously and often find themselves returning to the countries of their birth when they retire or wish to set up a home base somewhere.

• *The scholar expat*

Feng studied mechanical engineering in Shanghai and gained some work experience with a German company in China after graduation. After three years in the workplace, Feng felt the need for further education and enrolled for a Master's programme in Germany with the support of her former employer. Her studies kept her in Germany for three years. She met and married a German and still lives in Germany today.

Scholar expats often return to their home countries after their studies are completed – sometimes because visa requirements and red-tape don't allow them to stay on. Some *scholar expats* find local employment in the countries where they have studied and stay on for several years or forever.

• *The entrepreneurial expat*

Marie had a flourishing business in France and had always wanted to live in Spain for a longer period of time. Fluency in Spanish and her studies in Spanish culture and philosophy, made her relocation to Spain less challenging than it could have been. Financial security and investment opportunities allowed Marie to set up a branch of her French business in Madrid. After three years, Marie returned to France leaving behind a successful branch of her business run by a local partner.

Entrepreneurial expats often spend periods abroad setting up branches of existing companies or setting up something completely new in the country of their choice. These range from mobile sausage-selling stalls to production plants for complex engineering parts.

• *The end-of-work-era expat*

Simone (65) and Stefan (67) had seen all three of their children relocate to Florida in the USA. Their careers over and retired, they sought additional happiness in being able to spend more time with their children and grand-children. In addition to that, they were not happy spending so much time indoors because of the long, cold winters in Finland and went off in search of more sunshine. Florida, as the sunshine state, seems to be a popular destination for foreign pensioners like Simone and Stefan.

End-of-work-era expats often remain in the country they relocate to and only seldom return to the country of their birth.

1.2 Where expats are going

So who's going where and why are they going there? I can't help but think here of a few lyrics from the Cole Porter song he wrote in the 20s, *Let's do it*. Porter sang about falling in love, but some of his lines apply equally well to what's happening with the migration of people today. As Porter wrote way back then: "*In Spain the best upper sets do it, Lithuanians and Letts do it… the Dutch in old Amsterdam do it, not to mention the Finns; Folks in Siam do it… some Argentines, without means, do it…,*", and so on.

Right now, there is no doubt that "*everybody's doing it*". People are moving, planning on moving or being moved. Global migration is commonplace and on the rise.

1.2.1 World migration in figures

A joint report[1] in October 2013 on world migration in figures by **OECD** (Organisation for Economic Co-operation and Development) and **UNDESA** (United Nations Department of Economic and Social Affairs), casts some light on current migration trends.

- Some 232 million international migrants are living in the world today.

- About half of all international migrants reside in ten countries. In 2013, the United States of America hosted the largest number of international migrants (45.8 million or 20% of the global total), followed by the Russian Federation (11 million), Germany (9.8 million), Saudi Arabia (9.1 million),

---

1   World Migration in Figures © OECD-UNDESA October 2013

the United Arab Emirates and the United Kingdom (7.8 million each), France (7.5 million), Canada (7.3 million), Australia and Spain (6.5 million each).

- In 2013, international migrants accounted for nearly 11% of the total population in the developed countries, up from less than 9% in 2000.

- Despite the economic and financial crisis, global migration continues to rise.

- The number of tertiary educated immigrants in OECD countries increased by 70% in the past decade to reach 27 million in 2010/11. About 4.7 million, or 17%, of them arrived in the past five years. This trend is mostly driven by Asian migration as more than 2 million tertiary educated migrants originating from this region arrived in OECD countries in the past five years.

- In 2010/11, about 100 million persons aged 15 years old and over were living outside their country of birth in OECD countries. This represented a 36% increase from its 2000/01 level and a 9% increase in comparison with 2005/06. In 2013, the global number of young migrants reached 34.8 million.

- Refugees account for a relatively small proportion of the global migrant stock. In 2013, the total number of refugees in the world was estimated at 15.7 million, representing about 7% of all international migrants.

The Chinese version of the World Migration Report 2013 published by the International Organization for

Migration and translated by the Center for China and Globalization, was officially launched in May 2014. According to this report, the number of Chinese emigrants rose to 9.34 million by the end of 2013, with the United States, Canada, Australia and New Zealand being the top four destinations. With more than 9 million planning to pack their bags, China has the fourth highest levels of emigration globally after India, Mexico and Russia, the report says. Most of the prospective migrants from China are middle-class people aged between 35 and 55.

The facts and figures leave no doubt that "everyone's doing it". What is not so apparent is why people are emigrating and immigrating elsewhere. A closer look at why reveals a host of reasons.

- As seen in the figures just given, despite popular belief, refugees and asylum seekers still represent just a small proportion of international migrants, but as world peace remains evasive, these numbers are set to increase.

- Companies continue to expand worldwide, not only in terms of their product and service platforms, but also in their organisational structures – expatriates and global businessmen and women are the order of the day for most international companies. Organograms today are littered with "worldwide" positions – Global Commodity Leader, International Quality Manager, Head of Purchasing: Worldwide, Global Supply Chain Manager, Head of International HR and so on. As global business continues to expand, work forces are becoming increasingly diverse and multicultural. International satellite branches are set up daily and service providers and suppliers are under increasing pressure to show an international presence before contracts are awarded.

- An integral part of such international expansion is what I like to call the "expat entity". Not only do companies employ staff members from several nations at one site, they also regularly send expats abroad for short-, medium- and long-term assignments. Most large companies also have short-term job-rotation and exchange programmes for both staff and interns. A recent report by market research and financial consultancy company Finaccord found that the number of expatriates across the world is at a record level, and growth is expected to continue over the next few years. The "Global Expatriates: Size, Segmentation and Forecast for the Worldwide Market"[2] report states that there are roughly 50.5 million expats worldwide, and the figure is expected to reach 56.8 million by 2017, or 0.77 per cent of the total global population. Over the past five years, there has been a compound annual growth rate of 2.4 per cent. According to the report, most expats – 73.6 per cent – are individual workers.

- Nearly five million international students are likely to be studying for degrees outside their own countries in 2014 in what has become a modern mass movement. Compared with the year 2000,

---

2 "Global Expatriates: Size, Segmentation and Forecast for the Worldwide Market", (2014) Finaccord Ltd

when 2.1 million students left home to enrol in a foreign college or university, the number has increased by a phenomenal 140%, an average of 10% every year.

Moving abroad is a serious step which requires a lot of preparation. Contrary to what many people believe, ensuring that your stint abroad is a positive and rewarding one, takes more than just a bit of bureaucracy and learning the local lingo.

CHAPTER 2
INTERCULTURAL COMMUNICATION

When once the decision has fallen that you are going abroad, one of your first thoughts may be about the language spoken. As English is still the lingua franca of our time, most speakers of English feel content that they can get by with that. Expats headed for China and those who can also speak Chinese will feel more confident that they will manage things in China well. Others will be trying to learn at least the basics or a few common phrases of the target language and will be attending language courses often sponsored by their companies. Unfortunately, many expats think that mastering a foreign language makes them masters of intercultural communication. Speaking the local language of the country you are going to live in is helpful, but successful intercultural communication is about much more than language skills – it's about mastering cross-cultural skills. To explain this in a little more detail, I would like to take a closer look at the words "intercultural communication".

2.1 The terms defined

Paul Watzlawick (July 25, 1921 – March 31, 2007) was an Austrian-American family therapist, psychologist, communications theorist, and philosopher.

Possibly one of his most famous claims is that "one cannot not communicate and that every behaviour is a form of communication". Watzlawick contended that it is impossible not to communicate and that even if communication is being avoided, that is a form of communication. Facial expressions, or even being silent, can be analysed as communication by a receiver. Have you ever noticed how when some people walk past beggars, they specifically try to avoid eye contact? What they are in fact communicating is, "I don't want to look at you, because I don't particularly want to talk to you or have you talk to me".

Communication is a means of connecting people or places and a means for exchanging information.

Inter-, comes from the Latin word for "between". Can we then assume that intercultural communication simply means exchanging information between people of various cultures? That would be an easy conclusion, but what exactly is "*culture*"? A quick search on Google reveals countless pages of definitions of culture and they all seem to have some kind of merit – none of them can be said to be wrong. Ask anybody that you know and they'll have a go at translating the term. Some people will define it in terms of common or learned behaviour and traditions. Others will define it in terms of food, music, clothing and religion. And some will define it in terms of political and social systems. All of these would be right in part. *Culture* is a word that has lots of different meanings. As far back as 1952, Alfred Kroeber and Clyde Kluckhohn compiled a list of **164** definitions of "culture" in *Culture: A Critical Review of Concepts and Definitions*.

A phrase I particularly like and that I think sums up the world "culture" very well is one coined by Geert Hofstede: "Culture is the software of the mind". Like software, culture is the programme that drives the hardware of different countries. Like software, culture is dynamic and quite regularly gets updates – updates that are often treated with suspicion and resistance initially. When once those updates have taken place and people have got used to them, they can no longer imagine life without them.

2.2 Some models of culture

2.2.1 The iceberg model of culture

(Beyond Culture (1976) by Edward T. Hall)

Culture is often compared to an iceberg which has both visible (on the surface) and invisible (below the surface) parts. Elements of culture which we can clearly see, such as food or clothing, are represented by the upper portion of the iceberg. These are the things that are immediately noticeable the moment you get to a new country – if you land at Dubai Airport, you cannot help noticing that many people are dressed in traditional clothing. Or if you drive in England after arriving from America, you almost immediately notice that people drive on the opposite side of the road. Those elements which are not as obvious, such as *why* someone eats or dresses the way they do, are represented by the much larger portion of the iceberg underwater. Failure to understand and recognise these parts of culture and the layers that compose them, as well as how they influence each other, is the main reason misunderstandings occur between people of different cultures. We only need to think about the

Titanic on its maiden voyage to know how dangerous this lack of knowledge can be.

2.2.2 The cultural onion

Another of Geert Hofstede´s cultural models, the "cultural onion", is a very simple model to help us understand the culture of a country. In his view, "culture" is like an onion: a system that can be peeled, layer by layer, in order to reveal the content. Imagine the whole onion as "culture" and as you peel the layers back, you see different levels which work on and influence culture in any society.

The core represents the values of a certain culture, which are slow to change and are heavily influenced by the history of that country or culture. Even if something seems to be outdated, it can still subconsciously play a role in a modern society. In the centre of the onion are the underlying values and cultural assumptions which influence all of the other layers. These beliefs, norms and attitudes are much harder to recognise without a deeper analysis and thorough understanding of each of these layers and how they interact. These "values" are how people believe things "ought to be", what they consider sacred and special to their culture. This level is invisible and is manifested through the three other layers: symbols, rituals and heroes.

– Rituals and traditions: The first layer around the core is described as "rituals". These are things you can usually see, hear, touch, smell or taste. A ritual can be, for example, eating habits (chopsticks are often used in Asia and knives and forks in most western cultures). In Portugal a kiss on the cheek twice is a common way of greeting, whereas in parts of Switzerland, a three-time-on-the-cheek kiss is common.

– Heroes: A hero can be a fictitious person, a national hero, a top sports personality or a television presenter – any person that is admired or seen to be a role model for other people in that society. Examples that come to mind are Mahatma Gandhi and Nelson Mandela.

– Symbols: These are words, artefacts, pictures that carry a special meaning for particular societies. One example is a word such as "*Ubuntu*" in South Africa, which refers to the essence of being human. Ubuntu speaks particularly about the fact that you can't exist as a human being in isolation. It speaks about the interconnectedness of people and it also means "I am what I am because of who we all are".

2.3 Expecting the unexpected

Having a basic knowledge of communication and culture and the ability to speak a language understood by some people in the host culture, will go a long way to easing your entry into the new country. Really settling in and feeling totally at ease, though, is a bit more complicated than the basics.

You should work on developing intercultural skills. You should be able to interact with the people from your new culture without automatically falling back on your own cultural assumptions – even if this means adopting an outlook that you may not always share. And more importantly, be prepared for surprises. No matter how much you learn about intercultural communication, never assume that you can actually reduce a culture to the models, tips, and guidelines meant to support strangers. Cultures are not uniform and you will encounter many regional differences that stem from a range of different factors. Let's take Germany for example. You studied German at university for four years and are confident that the language will not be a problem – until you arrive in Lower Bavaria, that is – where you will be working for the next three years. You will soon notice that although all Germans can speak and understand the school German that you were taught, most of them naturally speak the Lower Bavarian dialect, which you cannot understand at all. This will lead to initial frustration as you always find yourself having to ask people to "please speak 'normal' German". In time, you too will understand the dialect and probably find smatterings of it in your own use of German.

To get the most out of your expat experience, you need to break out of your comfort zone and immerse yourself in the local culture. Letting go of initial impressions, hearsay and stereotypes is a good start. Making the transition from "living like an expat" to "living like a local" takes time. For most people, some aspects of the local culture seem strange at first but are accepted as simply being different and even interesting or amusing in a pleasant way. After living in your new host country for a while, little things that you initially considered charming may begin to irritate you. You will then start to make comparisons with the way things were back home. An expat from France was highly irritated when he discovered that the little town he had chosen to live in only had a very slow internet connection and that he would no longer be able to livestream films in his native language – his expectation was that in a first world country such as he was in, a fast internet connection would be available no matter where he lived.

When you feel frustrated, try to be respectful and patient. Remember that expats are guests in host cultures and should act accordingly. In time, not only you will learn to accept and deal with those very things that initially drive you crazy, you may find that the host culture starts to take on some aspects of the culture that you have brought with you. When I first came to Germany, it surprised me that hardly anybody drank tea with milk. After 16 years in the country, many people in my circle of friends and acquaintances ask me to make them "that lovely tea with milk in it". So, hang in there!

CHAPTER 3
READY, STEADY, GO

Moving, at the best of times, is not for the timid. This is the part where you'll realise that knowing the language and a few dos and don'ts is handy, but for ease of entry into your new country, you need a lot more information and, more importantly, a lot more patience and the right attitude. Without the right attitude, even the best laid plans for moving overseas won't get you far. You need to remain calm and focused when you are making your preparations for going overseas and try not to let the stress get the better of you. A good tip is to work with to-do lists and sense the progress you are making as you tick off item after item as done.

3.1 The physical move

Moving abroad requires organisational expertise and the determination to become "au fait" with the bureaucratic requirements of your chosen host country. Perhaps you are lucky enough to be an *everyday expat* and have the support of an experienced international HR team that can guide you through some of the initial difficulties such as organising visas and work permits. If you're going it alone, you need to be thorough, careful and patient when faced with red tape and an endless number of forms to complete and certified documents to provide. Bureaucracy is not country-specific – it's everywhere and will be with you on many parts of your overseas endeavour. Rather than cursing and berating it, see it as your companion and as your direct link to living right.

Be prepared for the emotional rollercoaster ride that the prospect of living abroad will take you on. The ups and downs you may feel are completely normal. Between packing crates, applying for visas, and storing or selling those possessions you can't take with you, there is very little time. If you are being accompanied by a partner and/ or children, things will seem worse, because every part of the group that's going abroad has its own agenda, its own concerns and its own idea about how things should be on the other side.

3.1.1 Pre-departure preparation

Look-and-see trip

If time and money allow for it, do visit the country you're planning to live in before you actually set off. It is also a good idea to link up with a local relocation agency for some initial orientation advice. Such agencies specialise in dealing with "expat issues" and can usually offer useful advice concerning finding accommodation, schooling, banking, local telecommunications and a host of other facilities. During such a look-and-see trip, gather important information on your host country and the pros and cons of living there. Also use this trip to learn more about the city you will be living in and try to talk to local people about things such as safety or water conditions. In some countries you should not drink tap water as it may be bad for your health. Use your look-and-see trip as an opportunity to build your own local network which will make life in your new host country much easier. Take a to-do list with you and tick the boxes as you go along.

My things or theirs?

In the preparation phase before you leave, one of the most important decisions to be taken will be whether you relocate all your belongings as well, or whether you take the option of furnished accommodation in the country you're going to and merely take essentials and personal items. Bear in mind that it is a comfort having some familiar things around you when you first move into new accommodation. Depending on where you're going, you may also be quite shocked at the difference in price and availability of certain items compared with home. Friends of mine who went to South Africa from Germany were disturbed to see that there was a choice of only four fully-automated coffee machines when they were looking for a new one. In Germany, it was quite common to have a choice of at least 50 different coffee machines. If you're travelling with children, it is a great comfort for them to have their own beds and familiar trappings from their former homes as they settle into their new ones. My suggestion for an expat trip anywhere over 18 months, would be complete relocation or at the very least a mixture of the new and the old. If you have a comfortable TV chair that you love relaxing in after work, and if it is possible, pop it into the container and relax in it as soon as it arrives. This is sure to put a smile on your face and a warm feeling in your tummy.

Utilities, phone, and Internet cancellation

Before packing your bags and moving to another country, do not forget to contact your utilities companies and cancel your contracts for electricity, water, gas, refuse removal and the like. Remember to get in touch with your phone company and your internet service provider as well before moving to another country. Even if your contract with them has not ended yet, you might be able to cancel it on the grounds of your leaving the country. You should in any case find out if this is possible to avoid unnecessary costs. In all of these cases, you may receive a final bill that you need to pay, either before your move or from abroad.

Cancelling subscriptions and forwarding mail

These are the last few details that you should straighten out before moving to a foreign country. If you have any subscriptions or regular deliveries, you should notify all these providers that you are leaving the country. To make sure the mailbox at your old place won't overflow with your personal mail, contact your post office and request them to forward your mail to the new address you are moving to.

Travelling by plane

Most often, the international airport in your country of choice will be your first stop on the road to expat living. At this point, you may have already endured a long flight, cramped into a seat between two strangers for countless hours. The arrival at the airport can be especially hard for those who have never been abroad for a longer stay and don't know how to travel with a lot of luggage. Don't worry though; with enough preparation nothing should go wrong.

Make sure to keep essential items such as medication, clean underwear, a toothbrush and your passport and visa documents in your carry-on luggage. Also, keep your host country's customs regulations in mind when you pack your suitcase. Some of your more personal items may be completely unproblematic in your home country, but in your host country they might raise some eyebrows at the local customs or even get you in serious trouble. In some countries, it is strictly forbidden to bring particular foods into the country and in New Zealand, for example, something as simple as a half-eaten banana will create unexpected and unpleasant questions on your arrival. Be sure to find out what your chosen country's sensitivities in this respect are and respect those for ease of entry into your host country.

Things you're going to miss

Before you get where you're going, think about items that you use often and would not like to give up while you are abroad. These are usually very simple things such as a particular brand of shampoo or toothpaste that you like and use. Before I left for Germany, I went on a huge shopping spree for cosmetics and underwear from Woolworths in South Africa, because I had heard that there was no Woolworths in Germany and couldn't bear the thought of having to change a brand of body lotion that I l loved and had been using for years. After a few weeks in Germany, I was told by locals that "of course we have Woolworths, but many of their things are very low quality and it's not a very popular store here in Germany." Quite downhearted, I headed for the nearest Woolworths to see if that was true. I was quite relieved to learn that Germany didn't in fact have "my Woolies" – the one that's equivalent to Marks and Spencer's in England – they had a Woolworth, an American chain that was nothing like the Woolworths I knew back home. Within a few months of my arrival in Germany, the chain went bankrupt and is no longer to be found in the country. Many of my English friends really miss their simple supermarket brand of tea when they're abroad and even though their host countries offer them an array of different teas, it's the good old common supermarket brand in a common kitchen cup that they most desire. Think too about reading matter, especially if you are going to a country where English is not the official language and you like to read in your mother tongue. It's a good idea to take a few books and magazines along for the first few weeks. Of course, things are a bit easier now with ebook downloads available pretty much everywhere for reasonable prices.

The import of medication, alcohol, food and firearms is often restricted or prohibited altogether. Be sure to get prescriptions and permits for all those potentially "awkward" items you don't want to leave at home. Declare any unusual amounts of prescription medicines at customs so that you have no problems right at the start. For most Americans, it comes as a real surprise that one cannot simply go into a store in Germany and buy a bottle of aspirin. Even though aspirin is commonplace and frequently used in Germany, you can only get it, even a mere strip of ten tablets, from a pharmacy. Do your homework and talk to people and ask about anything that comes to mind as "special" to you and that you would not want to be without in your first few expat weeks.

Precious pets

Always check the laws and regulations for importing and exporting domestic pets from your home country to your new country. This information is usually published on the website of the government agency dealing with animal and plant control. Importantly, not only do requirements for pet importation vary widely from country to country, they also vary widely depending on the type of pet you are importing, and the country where the pet is coming from. Generally speaking, your dog or cat will require a veterinary certificate showing that all vaccinations are up to date – especially rabies – and that deworming has been done within the past six months. Some countries, such as the United States, also require a wellness certificate issued by a certified veterinarian four to seven days before travel stating that the animal is in good health. Many countries require the quarantine of cats and dogs at the pet owner's expense. Do also check with your veterinarian and the relevant domestic government agency for any additional exportation or re-importation requirements. If you travel back home with your pet for holidays, be sure you have all the paperwork you need for re-entry. For example, if you are travelling from the European Union, make sure your veterinarian issues you an EU Pet Passport and that your domestic pet is microchipped for re-entry. Find out well in advance what the country regulations are regarding the import of pets.

Paying your way

Changing money before you arrive is always a good idea. You can, of course, still change money at the airport if you are in desperate need of cash. It is a lot more expensive, though, and you should only do it in case of an emergency. Nowadays, credit and even international debit cards serve you well in almost any country. It's not a bad idea to have a little bit of cash for little things such as getting a trolley at the airport or tipping a taxi driver or porter.

Hey ho, hey ho, it's off to work you go

No matter what is behind your decision to move to a new country, you should have at least some work opportunities lined up before you take off. Of course, if you are a student with a study permit and a place at a tertiary education institution, a pensioner with a good pension, or if your company wants you to move abroad for a special assignment, you don't have to worry about this part!

In all other cases, you should familiarise yourself with the job market in your destination of choice and see whether your qualifications are actually in demand and whether they are recognised by local administrative authorities. As a qualified and experienced high school teacher from South Africa, I was shocked to learn that my bachelor's degree and teaching diploma were not recognised as sufficient by German education authorities and that I was not allowed to teach in a government school without taking the German "Staatsexamen" and that would have meant going back to university for a further two years. For this reason, I chose the self-employment route, but for that too, do your research thoroughly to familiarise yourself with the implications relating to tax, social service contributions and the like.

If you're the more adventurous expat who wants to go job hunting after arrival in your country of choice, you really should do a bit of homework before you leave. This route can be risky and it may take quite a while before you start earning sufficient money to cover all your expenses, so be sure to have a little nest egg tucked away for those first weeks or months. After all, a steady income is important to prevent your new dream from becoming a nightmare.

3.1.2 Post-arrival plans

The first step towards your expatriate life is leaving the airport and heading for your new, temporary accommodation. Ensuring your safe transportation from the airport to your accommodation is essential. No matter whether you are staying at a hotel, a hostel or whether you have already rented your own place, you should know how to get there safely. Unless you have family members or friends in your host country who can pick you up at the airport and take you to your new home, you will have to find other means of transportation. Many hotels offer free or cheap airport shuttle services. Contact your hotel before you leave and ask for the most convenient way to get there. They will be able to provide you with information. Another option would be to use public transportation or licensed taxis. Find out in advance about how to recognise licensed modes of transportation, as this ensures a certain safety standard and set transportation fees.

Waiting for your things

No matter where you have chosen to go, the first few days after arrival are often the most daunting. If you have taken a flight halfway around the world, you are probably very tired and even jet-lagged. Be kind to yourself and allow a little space for your soul – try to relax and get some rest. You'll have time to really settle in, so take things one step at a time in so far as you able. The fact that you are in your new country for an extended stay may take a while to sink in, so allow for that.

It can take quite a while until the container with your belongings finally arrives at your new home. Maybe you even left some of your household goods in storage or sold them before you left home. Until your things arrive, you may want to get a few things to make life immediately more comfortable and might well even find a few local items that appeal to you. Go exploring and take a trip to local stores to see what's on offer and to get an initial idea of what things cost. You'll definitely find one or two little things and can immediately give your new home a bit of local flair and your own personal touch. Buy a map of your new home town and take little walks, drive around or explore the area by public transport. You will soon find shops and cafés in your neighbourhood that you like and could already start meeting new people and learning about new things to eat and drink. It took me only one coffee bar visit in Porto to learn that when I asked for a Café Latte, I didn't get what I expected. After taking a photo of it with my mobile telephone, I was able to show the next waiter what I wanted and promptly got the answer, "Ah, Galão!" *and* the drink that I wanted.

Do not hesitate to ask for help or directions. That way you will quickly get in touch with the locals. Familiarise yourself with local public transport possibilities and use them to familiarise yourself with the area without having to concentrate on driving a car yourself. Your new home town is just waiting to be discovered in more detail.

Get connected

Getting connected is essential to let your loved ones at home know that you are safe and sound. Especially during the first few days, it will help you to be able reach out to your usual support system and to get their support in the first, often uncertain, days. If you do not want to sign a mobile phone or internet contract right away, you can get a prepaid card for your mobile phone instead. It is quite a convenient option and allows you to be flexible. If your host country is using the same system as your home country, you may even be able to keep using your mobile phone SIM card from home. Be careful with this option, though, as this can get really expensive even if you are only using basic services such as phone calls and text messaging. To use the internet, try to figure out if there are any Wi-Fi hotspots available. Many cafés, libraries or public places offer wireless internet access free of charge, so make sure to bring your smartphone, pad or laptop along. These will be your comforters too when you are feeling a bit down or homesick and want to hear familiar voices and see familiar faces and places. There is nothing quite like a Skype call from your mum's or sister's kitchen directly to yours – these are the moments that will guard your sanity when things get tough and you're starting to feel that you've had enough.

CHAPTER 4
SURVIVING EXPAT EXHAUSTION AND CULTURE SHOCK

4.1 Expat exhaustion explained

Only a few months had passed since a close friend of mine had started her expat assignment when I received a depressed-sounding and emotion-filled message from her saying that she hated the city she was in, she hated the food, she hated the people and quite frankly she just wanted to get out of there and get back home. Though this message was a bit dramatic at the time and she did complete (without any extension to the agreed period, though), this kind of response is not uncommon in expat life. Expats sometimes get fed up – or what I like to refer to as "expat exhaustion" – and want nothing more than to return to what they perceive to be normality and the ways of the world that they previously understood and loved.

Expat exhaustion can come along at virtually any stage of the expat experience – it can start a few weeks after arrival at your destination, a year or two into your assignment or shortly before you are going back home anyway. If you have been frustrated but have managed to keep your feelings in check, your patience and tolerance levels will decrease the closer it comes to the end of your assignment – perhaps because then you know it is no longer necessary to MAKE things work. Some people do not experience it at all. Regardless of whether, or when, or even the intensity with which it hits, what seems to be consistent is that expat exhaustion is characterised by an overwhelming feeling of being tired of the expat experience and the desire to leave.

4.2 Strategies for coping

Identify the root of the problem

This may be difficult to pinpoint immediately, but with a bit of introspection you may be able to identify and analyse what it is that really bothers you, and where the underlying problem has its roots. Do you hate your job? Do you dislike your country to the point where it is intolerable to continue living there? If the answer to both is yes, how would it affect your future goals if you choose to leave earlier than planned? These are important questions to ask. All too often, though, expat exhaustion is caused by less obvious issues such as having a problem with local telecommunications, having an isolated yet frustrating encounter with a local person, or something as simple as not being able to find an English newspaper to read. If any of these, or similar things, are causing you to feel fed up and exhausted, consider whether there is something you can do to improve these situations or whether you can find alternatives to replace them with.

Have a change of scenery

Sometimes just a change of scenery and getting away works wonders to lift your spirits. A day trip, or even a longer one if time and money allows for it, might be exactly what you need to get back on track. This may be a good time to go somewhere where you have a support group or person – a good friend or even a business acquaintance that may understand what expat life is all about. Even consider a brief trip home if you are really missing your family, friends, food, etc. Stock up on some comfort items and bring them back to your expat country.

Give the place you live in another chance

Get out on the streets where you live. Make it your business every time you go out to find at least one new thing, place, activity, food or drink and try it out. Talk to someone you haven't talked to before – even the local newspaper seller or bus driver would react pleasantly if you were to simply greet them enthusiastically and ask how they're doing. It's OK to get stuck in your comfort zones if that makes you happy, but get out of it as soon as you start feeling that you're reaching breaking point and look for new motivation and inspiration.

Get moving

There is nothing like a bit of physical activity to top up on some feelgood factor. Join a fitness class, go for a walk or even clean your flat to booming music with an energetic beat. There is a lot of scientific evidence to prove that exercise helps to lift your mood and give you an energy boost. Get out and breathe in some fresh air and soak up the impressions on the outside of your apartment.

The power of positive thinking

Try to be around positive people that make you feel the same. Don't fall into the trap of joining forces with another unhappy expat and singing your songs of woe together. Create a "positive diary" and write down three things that were positive every day. It's a good idea to do this shortly before going to sleep, because it forces you to end your day focussing on the positives and eliminating the negatives and frustrations. Going to sleep with positive thoughts is a good basis for waking up with more of the same.

Be nice to yourself

Don't be too hard on yourself. What you're feeling is OK and quite normal, because you are who you are. Even though other people may feel differently about the issues that bother you, that's because they are different from you. As long as you try to counter the feelings you have with positive, solution-oriented thoughts, things will pick up and there will be brighter days. And have some "do nothing" moments – expats often try to do too much in too short a time – be kinder to yourself and reward yourself with "do nothing" moments. Those are also very good for the soul.

4.3 Culture shock – the phases

And then there's culture shock – a phrase often used rather humorously when people report on strange things they encountered on holidays or short business trips. Culture shock is in fact a serious phenomenon and something all expats should at least be aware of. Even if you do not suffer from culture shock yourself, a family member, an acquaintance or even a colleague may suffer from it and it's a good thing to be prepared and be able to recognise the symptoms and know some possible strategies for coping with and getting to grips with it. As an expat, you are unlikely to escape it completely. Its effects can be severe, and in some cases they are even responsible for expat assignments being terminated prematurely. Not everyone goes through all the well-known stages. While some skip stages or rush through them, others may experience certain stages of cultural transition more than once and in a different order. Culture shock can be a rather stressful, nerve-racking phenomenon, but it is an essential part of the transition process and the willingness to work through it is the first step towards integration.

Stages of culture shock

Most expats go through various stages of culture shock before they finally adapt to the way of life in their host country. Knowing what these stages are will help you recognise and deal with them appropriately. Most experts define culture shock as a curve-like process while many people who have experienced it first-hand say that it manifests itself in a series of waves. Positive and negative feelings often take turns and make expats feel as though they are on an emotional rollercoaster ride.

The honeymoon phase

The honeymoon phase is the first of four culture shock stages. It's that phase when expats still experience their time abroad the way most tourists do. Excitement runs high, there are lots of new, exciting things to discover and even the odd things are seen with amusement, tolerance and enthusiasm. Most expats don't even realise that what they are experiencing is the first of several stages.

Janine D has just arrived in Hong Kong and is in temporary accommodation – a five-star hotel – until she finds her own apartment. The streets are full of people, the weather's warm and pleasant having left her home country in the midst of winter. People are friendly, happy and enthusiastically support her with any uncertainties she may be feeling. It seems as if nearly everybody speaks English and it is far easier to communicate with people than she thought. The city is vibrant, there is always something going on and she feels quite excited at the prospect of being there for the next two or so years. After quickly popping into the office she'll be working in, she was pleasantly surprised at how friendly and helpful everybody was. The honeymoon phase usually only lasts a few weeks for expats like Janine and then life gets down to "daily business".

The frustration phase

This second phase comes after the honeymoon phase when the daily grind begins to catch up with expats and most begin to recognise how their host country differs significantly from their home country. They focus mostly on the little things they miss and on conflicts arising from cultural misunderstandings. Janine D enlisted the help of a local property agent and, armed with what she believed to be a very generous accommodation allowance, she enthusiastically set off in search of a place to stay. Her allowance would certainly get her something quite exclusive and luxurious in a good part of town in her home country. Soon after viewing the first few apartments and rejecting them outright as either too small, too smelly, in a horrible part of town or poorly and too sparsely furnished, Janine D realised that her money was not going to get her what she expected and hoped for. As her search continued and she realised that decisions had to be made quickly if she DID want a particular place – accommodation was sought after in Hong Kong and quickly snapped up – Janine D started compromising and settled in the end for a place that was way below her quality and service expectations and way above her budget expectation. And she learned what furnished meant in Hong Kong – a furnished kitchen didn't automatically come equipped with an oven and a dishwasher. Loneliness, homesickness and isolation are characteristic of this phase. The frustration phase usually lasts between a few weeks and a few months, depending on one's personal fight against the unpleasant culture shock stages.

The adjustment phase

During the third stage of culture shock, expats usually begin to regain a sense of appreciation. They have now spent quite some time in the new culture and are slowly learning to understand the different way of life.

Janine D has learned to accept her accommodation and has found other things to be excited about. Regular shopping sprees to the many local markets stocked with goods that are sometimes unusual and always cheaply priced has lifted her mood and taken the focus away from the accommodation issue she faced in the first few weeks. This is the point when assimilation is starting to happen. Janine D is slowly learning to deal with everyday difficulties. For her it is getting easier to adjust to her new life as she is getting familiar with social customs and everyday life in Hong Kong.

The mastery phase

During the mastery phase, people begin to understand the similarities and differences between their home country and the new culture they are confronted with. They begin to accept and appreciate those very differences and the aspects which are unique to the culture of their host country. In the mastery stage individuals are able to participate fully and comfortably in the host culture. Mastery does not mean total conversion – it's merely coping with the culture and even adopting some aspects of it willingly. This can range from eating certain foods that seemed odd at the beginning or wearing colours that seemed outrageous or listening to music that would never have appealed to you before.

In the mastery phase, expats often gain a new sense of confidence, tolerance and flexibility. This is when they finally begin to feel at home in their host country and their journey through the various stages of culture shock has come to an end.

Reverse culture shock

It may come as a surprise that culture shock doesn't only affect those who are moving abroad. Expats who return home after a long period of living in another country may also find themselves confronted with it. This phenomenon is known as reverse culture shock. A certain nostalgia for the expat life style often combines with difficulties in re-adjusting to the way of life in one's home country to re-create the culture shock experience for returning expats. While there is little you can do to completely avoid it, there are certain techniques which will help you minimise its effects. Trying to fit back into your old circle of friends isn't always easy. It may take some time for them to accept that you have changed, and for you to accept that they have just got on with their lives. Getting in touch with some other "repatriates" who share your experience is a good way to get over any readjustment issues.

Minimising the effects of culture shock

Culture shock is not a myth, but a predictable phenomenon. Anybody who spends more than just a vacation abroad goes through it. The intensity with which people experience it, however, depends on a lot of factors. Those who receive the least support on a professional and personal basis are usually hit the hardest. Expat spouses in particular often feel isolated and resentful when they experience life in a new cultural environment. In order to avoid failed expat assignments and early repatriation, HR departments should support expats and expat spouses from the very beginning, e.g. in the form of intercultural competence training. Expatriates who organise their move abroad entirely on their own can also take measures to minimise the negative emotional effects caused by their relocation and try to soften the blow. If expats learn about the culture and people of their host country in advance, they will be less shocked by obvious differences in social customs, religion, language or food.

4.4 Transition shock

Culture shock is a subcategory of a more universal construct called transition shock. Transition shock is a state of loss and disorientation predicated by a change in one's familiar environment which requires adjustment. There are many symptoms of transition shock, some of which include:

- excessive concern over cleanliness
- feelings of helplessness and withdrawal
- irritability
- anger
- mood swings
- glazed stare
- desire for home and old friends
- physiological stress reactions
- homesickness
- boredom
- withdrawal
- getting "stuck" on one thing
- suicidal or fatalistic thoughts
- excessive sleep
- compulsive eating and drinking and subsequent weight gain
- stereotyping host nationals
- hostility towards host nationals.

CHAPTER 5
EXPAT HEALTH AND SAFETY

One of the greatest concerns for expats is whether they will have access to good medical care. Of course, those expats going abroad for their companies are usually insured sufficiently and have no cause for concern should they need health care – at least not from a financial perspective. Expats who are "going it alone" need to ensure that they have sufficient health cover to prevent dire financial need or, even worse, no access to care when they really need it. Independent insurance brokers are able to provide you with professional advice on the coverage you need. Before you sign up with a health insurance provider, make sure your policy covers your host country and that you are protected for your entire stay. The insurance provider of your choice should offer a toll-free service number where you can get support around the clock if necessary. Medical systems differ greatly from country to country, so this is an area that needs to be thoroughly researched before departure.

5.1 Different strokes for different folks

Be aware that what you are used to in one country may be very different in your new host country. Government health in most European countries is of a high standard and costs are rarely felt by the patients themselves – they and their families are either adequately insured by monthly contributions or medical care is a state-provided service for minimum cost. Even expats that have good insurance cover may have to deal with low standards of medical care.

Josef S developed an allergy while on an expat assignment in Beijing. Well-insured and with easy access to private medical care, he went to the local international hospital for assistance. He was most pleased to find a doctor who was also an expat from the same country as he was. After a diagnosis and treatment plan, he set off from the hospital confident that the allergy would soon be under control. To his dismay, it got worse, so he went back to the hospital, this time to a different doctor, who on seeing the tablets he was taking, recognised them as sleeping tablets and not the ones prescribed by his doctor on the previous visit. There had been a mistake in the dispensary. Although this can happen anywhere in the world, it is more common in countries where language inadequacies and misunderstandings make such errors more common.

Natalie D, close on 40 years old at the time, was astounded that she could not get the contraceptive pill without going through a battery of medical check-ups first. Although this is probably a good thing, it can be annoying when you don't have time and are used to simply popping into a local pharmacy and getting it over the counter without prescription. Different health standards and difficulties in getting medication are not the only threats to an expat's health. You might encounter tropical diseases which spread in warmer climates. Food and water quality are also an important factor when it comes to expat health. Healthy drinking water is not a given around the world and in countries such as China and Mozambique, large, dispensable 25-litre canisters of water are delivered on a regular basis to expat homes. This needs to become part of your "grocery" plan to ensure that the water you are drinking is safe. The hygiene standards in your host country may not quite compare to what you are used to. You may get sick after consuming something at a local market if your stomach has not "acclimatised" along with the rest of your body – hence the term "Delhi Belly" for visitors to India who are not used to either the stronger spices or grabbing a bite from a stand along the road as many locals do.

Sven B, an expat in China, had to end his assignment prematurely, because his stomach simply couldn't handle local cuisine and despite several courses of action he was in and out of hospital with ailments. On his return to his native country and after a few appointments with his local doctor, he had no further complaints of this nature.

5.2 Pre-departure check-up, vaccination and immunisation

Before you board a plane to travel to your new destination, think about your health. Visit your doctor for a thorough pre-departure check-up and find out which precautions to take for the country of your destination. If you have a pre-existing health condition, e.g. a severe allergy, prepare for situations related to your medical condition when you plan your expat life. It is extremely important that you are able to communicate your situation in case of an emergency. You can prepare yourself by learning words and key phrases to describe your specific medical problem in the local language. Knowing where and how to get your medication and what to say to medical personnel is essential. Apart from learning key phrases by heart, you should also write them down and carry a note in your wallet or pocket. Alternatively, you can try and find out whether there is any form of medical ID commonly used and recognised in your host country.

For some diseases there are preventative vaccinations which are vital parts of healthcare. Hepatitis A/B, typhoid, and malaria are common diseases which you can easily prevent by getting either the right immunisation or prophylactic medication. Contaminated food or water is a health issue many expatriates all over the world, especially in developing countries, have to deal with. It can cause minor gastro-intestinal infections. In some cases, however, it can even be the source of severe diseases such as cholera, typhoid, or hepatitis.

It may all sound a bit daunting to an expat just getting ready to go abroad, especially if they are going to be accompanied by children. Common sense and taking a few simple health precautions will go a long way to keeping your health good and eliminating cause for concern. Here are a few things to consider:

- Always wash your hands before and after handling food

- Use only bottled, boiled, or sanitized water

- Eat only fresh and thoroughly cooked food which is still hot

- It's better to err on the side of caution if you are unsure about the hygiene standards or the quality of food or water that you are being offered and avoid the following:

- Reheated food

- Drinks and food that have been cooled with ice (one doesn't know if the water used to make the ice was free of contamination)

- Uncooked fruit or vegetables, unless you can peel them yourself. Also avoid salads that have been rinsed in local water, as these are often just quickly rinsed under running tap water

- Food that has been exposed to flies

- Dairy products which are not pasteurized or have not been properly refrigerated

- Undercooked or raw seafood

5.3 Have important details at hand

The basis for a safe expat life is knowing what to do and where to go when things go wrong. Knowing where and how to get support will give you the necessary peace of mind. For that reason, create a list with important contact information you might need in case of an emergency. This list should include the telephone numbers of hospitals and English-speaking doctors (if you're not fluent in the local language), as well as the local emergency number. Note that numbers for calling the police, an ambulance or the fire brigade differ from country to country. The address and telephone number of your nearest embassy/consulate and a number to reach your health insurance provider should also be on this list so you're prepared for every eventuality. It is generally advisable to carry a medical insurance card with you at all times and the name and number of someone who could act on your behalf should you not be able to do so yourself.

5.4 General safety measures

General safety precautions differ greatly from country to country. Depending where you're going to and where you're coming from, you may have to behave differently from what you're used to. I remember coming to Germany from South Africa and being overly sensitive about safety compared to my German acquaintances. I was not used to living without being fenced in and setting alarms every time I left home. It bewildered me to see most houses without fences around them and people leaving expensive decorative articles and even garden furniture "unprotected" from theft. In time, I realised that the level of safety and security required in my home country was very different from that required in Germany. The danger is that one can become complacent and even irresponsible after long periods of not even petty crime.

Being safe in your host country is partly up to you. You are subject to the local laws and regulations and you need to know what you are allowed to do and what not. When it comes to the law, it's pretty much the same rule all over – ignorance is no excuse – even if you are not aware that something is against the law, you can still be punished for it, so take care that you are a law-abiding expat and stay out of trouble.

If you keep an eye on the local news and talk to local co-workers or neighbours, you should get a good sense of security threats and the political situation in your new home. Some countries are very stable while others face safety threats on a regular basis. A bit of common sense that most tourists practise goes a long way to staying safe in your host country – don't leave valuables lying around or display your wealth ostentatiously. As the old saying goes – never tempt a thief. Ask about no-go zones in your local area and avoid those. Be cautious and alert when you're out and about and be aware of your environment and of the people around you. Maybe the area you live in is perfectly safe and you have no reason to worry. In other neighbourhoods, however, it may be necessary to have barred windows and a locked front gate with an alarm system to keep your family safe and sound.

CHAPTER 6
FINANCE AND INSURANCE FOR EXPATS

When you move abroad, financial stability and financial planning are essential elements for your safety and success. A financial cushion is necessary to cover additional or unexpected costs. In a 2009 NatWest survey on moving to a foreign country, 87% of Brits thought that if they were to move overseas, they would be better off financially. In reality, depending on the country you are living in, several factors can make expat life even more expensive than at home. Even when you move overseas to a supposedly "cheap" country, life abroad can be more costly than you expect. In the beginning, immediately after you move overseas, you'll probably insist on the more expensive expat lifestyle with every amenity you know from home. Especially in third-world countries, the costs of maintaining a western lifestyle can be exorbitant. Either a willingness to adapt to the local way of life, or proper financial planning, are essential to ensure your expat experience is a success.

6.1 International payment methods

Credit, debit, pre-paid cards and traveller's cheques

Many people, particularly those who are only travelling abroad for a short time, prefer to use their credit or debit cards for every purchase or payment. This does not come as a surprise as it is a convenient and widely accepted payment method. Credit cards are particularly popular for everyday purchases as well as visa or car rental fees. While some card types are accepted in almost every country, there might be cases when your credit card just won't do the trick and you will need to get your hands on some cash instead. For withdrawals from an ATM, debit cards are the preferred international payment method. Unlike credit cards, you will not be charged interest if you withdraw money and the fees will be a lot lower.

Pre-paid cards, on the other hand, are a safe alternative to traveller's cheques. You can only spend the money you have previously put on the card. The card itself can be replaced if you lose it and the money on it is protected. The advantage of pre-paid cards is that they are not linked to your bank account. Thus, the money in your account is always safe. International traveller's cheques have been around for a while and are still a somewhat popular method of payment among travellers although they are a little outdated. They are available at your bank and at exchange bureaux, and come pre-printed with fixed amounts in all major currencies. They work in the same way as regular cheques: write the name of the person or store you are paying on the cheque and sign it. You might be asked to show proof of identity, so it is important that you keep your ID or passport at hand. Traveller's cheques are fairly safe and allow you to bring enough of a foreign currency without actually carrying a lot of cash. In case of loss, your bank can quickly replace them. Unfortunately, traveller's cheques are not a common payment method in every country.

Buying foreign currency

In some countries, smaller shops and restaurants in particular will not accept credit cards or cheques. Do some research beforehand to find out about the preferred payment methods and whether it makes sense for you to exchange money before you embark on your journey. After all, planning ahead is key when it comes to buying foreign currency. That way, you will have enough time to figure out which bank or exchange companies can offer you the best deal. Try to avoid the so-called bureaux de change at airports. They usually offer very bad rates and charge 10%–15% in fees. While cash is still the most reliable international payment method, it is also the one that's least safe. If your money gets lost or stolen, there is only a very small chance of retrieving it.

6.2 Taxation for expats

Find a good tax consultant and know what it is that you need support and advice on. And be fussy. Don't settle for the first person or company you find just because you are busy. Financial matters, like matters of personal health, should be entrusted to people you can fully rely on.

- Do you simply want someone to help prepare your tax return so you don't have to file your income taxes from abroad yourself?

- Do you need financial advice on tax planning for the expat life that lies ahead?

- Do you want someone who is familiar with the details of several different tax systems?

- Do you want to make sure that you are up to date with proper bookkeeping for your own business abroad?

- Do you already have some legal issues regarding international taxation, and want them to help you with the tax authorities?

Matters of international taxation can involve twice as many pitfalls as your usual tax return. Plenty of expatriates shy away from this issue with good reason. But if you start dealing with taxes for expats before you actually move, you'll save plenty of time later on – and perhaps some money, too! Most people dread the deadline for their tax form, and expats are no exception to that rule. However, when it comes to taxes for expats, filing them properly is especially important. In the worst case scenario, you might get into trouble in two countries, have bureaucratic problems to sort out in a foreign language, and end up paying more than expected, e.g. in the way of fines. The best case scenario, on the other hand, means saving money. While nobody likes actually dealing with the revenue service, everyone enjoys getting back some hard-earned income from the authorities. Taxes for expats depend on various personal circumstances, e.g. your country of origin and its tax system, your destination and its tax law, your residence for fiscal purposes, your marital status and number of children, as well as your individual finances.

Organise your paperwork

Try to find all documents that serve as proof of income (e.g. pay slips, bank statements, the tenancy agreement for a property you let). Moreover, try to think of everything that might grant you a tax deduction and document this too (e.g. medical bills, charity donations, private insurance plans, expenses for job-related seminars). Even if you need a professional to finalize your tax return, you won't get around this step – they will demand proper documentation too.

Get in touch with the tax office

As a next step, you ought to contact your local tax office and find out about the legal obligations for those moving abroad. The following checklist provides some questions you might want to ask:

- Do you have to file your taxes for the ongoing tax year when you leave? Or can/should you hand in your tax return for the entire fiscal year from abroad?

- Do similar regulations apply for returning to your home country?

- Have your country of origin and your destination agreed upon a tax treaty? Do you need to pay your income tax at home, abroad, or in both countries?

- Do you still need to file an annual tax return while living abroad? Or is doing your taxes overseas, with the local authorities, enough?

- Can you download the current tax returns online, or order them via mail?

- Where do you need to send your tax return? Does the usual address information still apply?

- Is there a special contact person for expats at your tax office back home? Make sure you know how to get in touch with them.

6.3 Introducing international banking

If you decide to open a new bank account prior to your departure, you should consider doing this with a global bank which offers services in your host country. Large international banks may even be able to help you open up a new account before or shortly after your move. Another important piece of information to know before you leave is what your withdrawal limit is. Will you have access to sufficient funds for the beginning of your international assignment?

Offshore or local banking?

One choice to make when it comes to international banking is whether you want to open an offshore bank account or a local bank account, or both. Offshore banking can give you easy access to your financial savings, but please keep in mind that these accounts may be inaccessible for some expats, as such banks often require you to make a high initial deposit and/or maintain a high minimum balance. The advantages of local banking include having somewhere for your salary to be deposited and being able to avoid the exorbitant ATM fees that are sometimes charged when you use a foreign card to withdraw money. Also, in some countries, you'll save money if you can use a local debit card when shopping online.

Your bank account back home

No matter what type of banking you decide is best for you, you will most likely also need to keep an account open in your home country. This makes sense if you are planning on returning to your home country at the end of your international assignment or still own property there. This account can be used to pay any expenses you still need to cover back home, such as mortgage payments or other outstanding loans. If you are living in a country which is politically or economically unstable, it is a wise decision to keep most of your wealth outside of this country, in accounts offshore and/or in your home country. You may even wish to transfer a portion of your earnings out of the country on a regular basis. It is also important to not have all of your savings in an account in your host country in case you fall victim to a scam or fraud during your time abroad. You will be pleased with your investment in international banking if such a situation should arise.

6.4 The cost of living an international life

Many expats or expats-to-be are interested in the cost of living they might be facing while working and living abroad. From utility to healthcare costs, here you can find an overview on what expenditure items to look out for when planning the budget for your own international experience. The actual move overseas is only the first step in an expat's experience. Once you have arrived, you will be facing not only a completely new work and living environment as well as a potentially very different culture and way of life, but in many cases also the use of a currency you have never handled before. In order for you to not be caught out by any unexpected costs, here is a list of typical expenditures. This way, you can check if you have forgotten any important items while planning your budget.

Housing and utilities costs

No matter where you end up living, costs for accommodation and utilities typically play a big role in your budget. Next to rent, you might have to pay an additional key deposit or security fee and utility costs are not to be underestimated either. You will have to factor in expenditure for water supply, sewage, electricity and gas for heating and/or cooking. Furthermore, you might be facing additional expenditure for communal services such as waste disposal. In any case, be sure to inform yourself as to whether it is your or your new landlord's responsibility to enter into a contract with utility service providers.

Communication and entertainment

Next to water and energy, many people nowadays consider an internet and telephone connection a basic need. Expatriates in particular use these to stay in touch with family, friends and acquaintances all over the world. Costs for such communication services can range from very cheap to extremely expensive, depending on where you are living or planning to live. If available, you might want to look into getting a package deal where you get your phone, internet and optionally also your television service from one single provider. Such bundles do usually cost less than the sum of their individual contracts and can also mean less of a hassle for you (e.g. only one technician visit for installation). When it comes to television and radio, you also need to be aware that in some countries you will have to pay a television and/or radio licence. Not only the majority of European countries, but also quite a few African and Asian ones, have such licence fees.

Buying groceries and general goods

Prices for groceries and general goods such as clothing and personal care products obviously depend heavily on where you are living as an expatriate. However, you can easily save money if you follow some simple rules. First of all, try to go for local goods and avoid imported products you might know from home. Such goods can cost quite a bit and you are often better off sticking with local offers, at least when it comes to everyday items. Another useful way to save money is to avoid eating out and to start cooking for yourself. While supermarket stores are often the place to go to in order to find products that do not cost a lot, you might also want to check whether your city has any local markets. There you can buy fresh and local produce for decent money and you might even have fun haggling for prices.

Healthcare expenditure

Many countries, such as Italy or Japan for example, have a good public health care system which often also covers you as an expat resident. Or you might be covered as part of your work benefits in your employment contract. However, if neither is the case, make sure you take out private health insurance before starting your new international life. Contact an independent insurance broker if you are feeling unsure about what coverage you need and want information on how much it is going to cost.

Costs for transportation

Transportation will surely also play a role in your budget. How big a role, however, strongly depends on the country and city you are living in. Prices for petrol alone vary greatly: in Kuwait, you will only have to pay approximately 0.168€ for a litre of petrol. In Norway, on the other hand, petrol is much more expensive and a litre can cost you around 1.877€. Around the world, you will encounter similarly varying costs for the upkeep of your own car or the use of public transportation services. With regards to your own car, keep in mind that the purchase and petrol are usually not the only expenditures connected to owning a car. Registration fees, car taxes and insurance, motorway tolls as well as regular mandatory checks of your car's safety are not unusual and can cost a pretty penny. Plus, very few cities can boast an abundance of parking spaces, so you might have to rent one for your car as well.

Further costs

Of course, the expenditure items listed above are not the only ones you will be facing while living abroad. If you have children you will surely encounter additional costs, for example in regards to their education: from everyday school material such as pens and paper to potentially high tuition fees for a private international school or university. And obviously we have so far also failed to mention any leisure activities that you might like to pursue. As with everything, whether your hobbies and favourite pastimes are affordable or not depends on where you are going to be living.

6.5 Essential insurance for expats

Insurance for motorists

Although the public transport system of your country of choice might be very good, you may decide to retain your independence by having your own car. For those expats supported by their companies, this is usually fairly trouble-free provided you have a valid driver's license. Apart from the driver's license, do ensure that you have valid motor insurance. It is even mandatory in some countries and can become really expensive in the event of an accident if you don't have it.

Motorists traveling within the EU don't need proof of car insurance at all. If you register a car in one EU member state and buy the legally required cover, all official policies include basic coverage for other member states by default. Only in case of accident do you have to produce your insurance papers. Though it is no longer mandatory as legal proof within the EU, the so-called Green Card remains the most easily recognised document for international drivers. Some other countries still expect foreign drivers to carry such a Green Card as proof of car insurance for border inspections or traffic police. These nations include: Albania, Belarus, Bosnia, Iran, Israel, Macedonia, Moldova, Morocco, Russia, Serbia, Turkey, and Ukraine. If you travel to one of these destinations, ask your local insurance company to issue you a Green Card beforehand.

Also find out which factors your premiums depend on and shop around. Here are some factors that may influence the price you pay:

- age

- the number of people that drive the car

- gender (The EU introduced unisex tariffs in 2012, but other countries might consider young male drivers a risk factor.)

- personal excess fees in the event of a claim

- where you keep the car over night

- the make and model of a vehicle

- driving experience and insurance record

The last point is something that surprised me – in an unpleasant way – when I first came to Germany. During the pre-departure phase, I applied for an international driver's license and so felt confident that I was legally allowed to drive in Germany. And drive I did – for a period of six months. I was then informed by another expat who had had a similar experience that I would have to get an official German driver's license if I planned to remain in Germany and wanted to continue driving legally on German roads. It made no sense to me that a country could allow someone to drive without limitation for six months and then require a change of license status. I thought that the first few months would be the most critical, especially as the expat tries to navigate their way around. I soon learned that my friend was right and that I indeed had to take a few lessons and a practical driver test with a local driving school – even though I had been driving accident-free for over 16 years. Don't let things like these get you down – just do what is required and get on with a happy life. Also remember that insurance companies aren't necessarily obliged to take your record from another country into account. Despite my former accident-free driving years, I was listed as a beginner driver in Germany, because the insurance companies calculated my driving experience years from the date that I got my German driver's license. Last but not least, be aware of when exactly the insurance coverage kicks in and when the premiums are due. In Germany, for example, motorists usually get temporary insurance papers for all travel involved in registering a car (e.g. driving it to the vehicle inspections office). Premiums are paid on an annual basis, but your car insurance company could make an exception and offer quarterly payments.

Of course there are further essential insurances for expats such as a general liability insurance to guard against personal accidents or mishaps. Life insurance may be an issue for some families as well. The best approach is to get professional advice, both pre- and post-departure to ensure that you are covered for all eventualities.

CHAPTER 7
THIRD CULTURE KIDS (TCKS) AND EXPAT CHILDREN

I grew up in South Africa with parents of Dutch and Irish heritage. In the rainbow nation with eleven official languages and as many different local peoples, I often grappled with what my true identity really was. Was I South African, or half Irish and half Dutch? Or half English and half Afrikaans? I often thought about my friend Natalia. She too was born in South Africa and grew up there exclusively. Her parents were from Portugal and in fact from two very different parts of the same country. Was Natalia South African or Portuguese? And so I often thought about what it is that gives us our identity. Today I no longer hold a South African passport and am a German citizen. Does that make me German? The answers to these questions, when put to different people, are different. I have decided that I am me – Marinda – South African born and a resident and citizen of Germany. Who I am is a combination of many factors, of which the countries of my birth and residence are only two. Did you grow up in one culture, your parents came from another, and you are now living in a totally different country? Then you are a third culture kid! That may sound like a lot of fun, but being a third culture kid is not always easy.

7.1 Third culture kids (TCKs)

The term "third culture kids" was coined in the 1960s by US sociologist Dr Ruth Hill Useem. She first encountered this phenomenon when she researched North American children living in India. These children spend many years outside their home culture, but never quite adapt to their host culture either. Caught between two cultures, they form their very own. While growing up as third culture kids may sound challenging, these children often benefit from their multicultural background. In general, they often achieve excellent academic results. About 90 per cent of them have a university degree, while 40 per cent pursue a postgraduate or doctoral degree. They usually benefit from their intercultural experience which helps them to grow into successful academics and professionals.

On the down side, a third culture kid (or TCK) may not be able to immerse themselves as completely into their new surroundings as expected. Instead, they may always remain an outsider in different host cultures. I remember Barbara telling me that she in fact resented her father more and more as she grew older. He was a civil engineer and although his many lucrative expat assignments left the family very well provided for financially, she attended 15 different schools in her life and always felt like the new outsider kid. She attended mostly international schools which was OK, because there were many other expat children there who could identify with what it felt like being the new kid in town. Barbara liked the fact that her English was excellent compared to children her own age back home where Dutch was her native tongue. And she liked the differences in the schools themselves – some had uniforms and offered many free-time activities which gave her the opportunity to mingle with other children and make friends fairly quickly. The problem was that Barbara never had her friends for very long before she was packing her new school bag for the next new school.

A particularly unpleasant phase in her schooling was when she had to attend a local school in America in a part of the United States that had no private international school. Here Barbara joined a school where the pupils had grown up near each other and known each other for several years. Very few of them even knew what an expat was, let alone an expat child. She felt lonely and isolated and was very unhappy until her father announced the next move. She always joked that she was nothing but an IBM kid – an "I'm being moved" kid – but deep down, the repeated loss of friends and things that were familiar to her, left her sad and lacking any sense of belonging. Even on short spells back home, she felt like an outsider in family circles and didn't ever get to know her cousins or the children in her neighbourhood. Barbara felt out of place when she returned to the country where she was born. Unlike local children her age, she didn't know anything about current TV shows, fashion trends, or the latest pop hits. This was a feeling she was exposed to every time she came home and every time she landed in a new country for another bout of expat life. Making new friends and saying goodbye to old ones will at some point become routine for a third culture kid. While this can be a way to create a network of friends all around the world, it may also lead to an out-of-sight-out-of-mind attitude. Although Barbara's intentions were good, she often had difficulties keeping in contact with former friends as she grappled more with the challenge of making new ones.

Thankfully, most third culture kids don't share Barbara's fate and get swept around the world on so many different assignments in just one childhood. While third culture kids must let go of their identity as foreigners when they return home, it is often the home country that can prove to be more foreign than anything encountered before. This often makes it hard for them to form their own identity. As adults, third culture kids very often move abroad again to work and raise their kids in a foreign country. Hence, third culture kids may end up raising third culture kids.

7.2 Supporting your children abroad

The most important thing is to give your child a sense of stability and consistency. When children get a sense of lacking cultural roots, they turn to their parents to find out which social and cultural rules apply. Family and home should always be a safe haven to a third culture kid. At the same time, it is important for your child to become familiar with their host country.

- *Learning foreign languages*

Encourage your children to learn the local lingo, even if they always use English as the lingua franca for schooling and initial contacts. Children learn languages easily and have fun showing off their newly acquired knowledge, especially when they communicate with people back home that don't know the new language at all.

- *Making friends*

For some kids, it is quite easy to make new friends. Others struggle to get in touch with children their own age. You can help your expat children by meeting other families in your new neighbourhood. Your HR department or people from your expat community may be able to help you with that. Organise play dates, join play groups or even have a welcome party and invite your new neighbours over. Remember that in some countries it is easier to get in touch with locals than in others. But as long as you don't give up, sooner or later you will make yourself at home in your new neighbourhood and your kids won't feel so foreign anymore.

- ### *Keeping in touch with home*

It is important for your expat children not to lose touch with people at home. You can help your children contact family members and friends at home frequently. Once you have set up an internet connection, you can show your children how to use online messengers, webcams, and programs such as Skype.

Also try to encourage your family and friends to visit you abroad. This helps expat children understand that these people have not disappeared completely but are in fact still a big part of their lives. Try to take a vacation once a year to visit your home country, too. A year can be a very long time for a kid. Visiting their home country and seeing the people they love can have a very comforting effect on expat children.

- ### *Give your expat kids some roots*

Celebrating your traditions is perhaps most important if you have expat kids growing up in another culture (the so-called third culture kids). It can help them keep one foot firmly rooted in their home culture, while also offering learning experiences that might not otherwise occur.

- *Back to school*

Choosing the right (international or local) school for your child is trickier than you may expect. It all depends on your child's fluency in the new language, on their age – younger children adapt more easily to their new environment – and on the duration of your international stay. If your child does not know the local language yet or if your assignment will last less than six months, you should consider a bilingual or international school. These schools not only offer an excellent education, they are also experienced when it comes to dealing with children leading an international life. This experience and the international student body can minimise the culture shock and help your child adapt. However, for a longer stay and if your children are still little or already know the local language, you should also consider a local public or private school. This way, your children will be immersed in the local culture and be able to acquire new – or improve existing – language skills. Thus, it will be easier for your kids to get settled and feel at home in a foreign environment.

7.3 Positive aspects of TCKs and expat children

Their experience abroad helps many third culture kids gain a greater understanding of cultural differences. Hebba was born in Egypt and since early childhood she has lived abroad, moving around with her expat parents every few years. At an early age, she realized that each country smells and tastes differently and that people around the world celebrate and pray in very different ways. She believes that it helped her become a more flexible and sensitive person.

Confidence and communication skills

Adapting to new situations quickly and with confidence is no problem for third culture kids such as Hebba. It is usually easy to adjust to new situations after being exposed to so many during childhood. Starting university in a new town away from former school mates would not be a particular challenge for most TCKs.

Excellent communication and diplomatic skills are what many third culture kids get out of their experience abroad. These skills help them thrive later on during their academic studies as well as their career.

Learning languages

Children pick up foreign languages easily, but do bear in mind that learning a language becomes harder for expat children the older they get. Many TCKs are multilingual.

CHAPTER 8
SUPPORTING YOUR SPOUSE AND FAMILY

8.1 The expat partner

Unless you are single and without close family ties, your decision to make a new home overseas will affect your partner, spouse, or family just as much as it affects you. You should never make the step of going overseas without including them. Many expat assignments fail because families are not seriously considered and often feel so frustrated that they simply want to return home. Although rare – and less likely to happen when younger, dependent children are involved – expat spouses have been known to return to their countries before the assignment in question has ended. If your spouse or family is not able or willing to accompany you when you go overseas, you will have to find a compromise. In about two-thirds of the cases in studies of "typical" expat assignments, the spouse's dissatisfaction is cited as the reason for returning home prematurely. In instances where your spouse does decide to go along with your plans of going overseas, don't forget to take their concerns seriously, and offer them your emotional support. Discovering a new foreign country together should be a positive challenge for your life as a couple, not an obstacle. Expat spouses often resign from their jobs or take long sabbaticals to accompany their partners on an assignment. This sacrifice should be treasured and respected to make it easier to deal with the low times that lie in store when an expat partner feels frustrated.

There are really only a few ways for expat spouses to deal with their partner's assignment abroad. They can either stay behind to continue life as they know it or they can "trail along". Both scenarios have their pros and cons. In each case, expat assignments can make or break a relationship or marriage. Travelling spouses often cannot pursue their own career while abroad and may experience some restrictions on their personal freedom. Thus, identity crises, due to the loss of their independence and status, are frequent. As most spouses of assignees statistically still tend to be women, local and cultural traditions may have a strong effect on their personal lives as well.

Anna G had a well-paid job and enjoyed what she was doing, but when her husband, Markus, was made a very good offer of an expat assignment in China for five years, she decided to give up her job and accompany him. In the beginning, everything was fine and Anna was very busy setting up the home and getting to know Shanghai and the many things the vibrant city has to offer. Supported by a large corporation and a professional relocation agency, there were very few difficulties to deal with in terms of the actual move and accommodation. Markus went off to work and was immediately part of a known and familiar network. Although he worked very long hours and often came home late, the couple spent their weekends exploring and getting to know their new home country. Anna was content and enjoyed the hustle and bustle and shopping opportunities that the big city had to offer. When once

Markus had settled into his new job and knew the ropes, he had to start travelling throughout the country. He was often away for four days a week and usually returned home late on a Friday night, completely exhausted and not in the mood for much else than a night on the couch. Anna, who by now had seen and done a lot in Shanghai, was starting to get bored and wanted to spend more time with people – and with Markus. She soon felt that she had done all the shopping she could think of and needed something else to stimulate her. The former business woman was becoming more and more frustrated by the day and soon wanted to return to the workplace. This was not as easy as she thought, because regulations governing expat spouse employment made it almost impossible for her to find a job, despite her excellent qualifications. Anna took her frustration out on Markus and soon found herself in the "poor victim" role. She resented having given up her independence and a good job back home and although the couple tried to come to terms with the situation, Anna decided to return to England. Once she was so unhappy about being without a job, she could no longer see anything positive about Shanghai. The vibrant, exciting city had become an "overcrowded mad house with millions of people pushing and shoving to get ahead".

The example above is a negative one and although it didn't have a happy ending for the couple, both Anna and Markus made remarkable strides in their careers. The example is not unusual though. On the upside, there are many expat couples and families who have a wonderful experience abroad and see their expat times as life-changing and fulfilling. For many couples, where both partners are working, an expat assignment is a perfect opportunity to plan in maternity or paternity leave. New parents are often very pleased at the prospect of being able to take time out to raise their children without too much financial sacrifice. Depending on the country you're leaving from, this could be a wonderful time for expat partners to enjoy their new countries and parenthood.

Be a team from the very beginning and remember that it's a decision you have made together. Particularly when things get more difficult and frustrations increase, stick together. There are local support groups in most countries and expat partners often help other expat partners to settle in and find a few instant and mostly well-meaning contacts – people either from home or from other countries, who, having already been through the relocation process, are always ready with advice or at the very least, are prepared to lend an ear. A move abroad is always a challenge and your partner will most likely go through the same highs and lows as you. It is important that you work together as a team and prepare this big step together. It pays in the end.

8.2 Strategies for staying happy

Don't isolate yourself – find a way to connect

Isolating yourself from your new culture is only going to reinforce your blues. Your spouse's career wasn't the only reason you moved abroad. What excited you about the opportunity to *become* an expat? Was it the sense of adventure? If so, how can you be more adventurous? Start out small. Buy an odd-looking vegetable from the grocery store or market and incorporate it into a dinner. Make friends with a local person. Having a friend who speaks the language can help you accomplish simple, daily tasks such as communicating with a handyman. More importantly, your friend may provide you with better insight into the culture you're living in and, perhaps, more of an appreciation for it.

Find and do something that fulfils you

Filling your days with household tasks can make the hours go by quickly, but won't provide you with the sense of satisfaction and achievement you used to get from a rewarding life back home. Some expat wives pick up long lost hobbies while abroad and others discover new ones. Start a new hobby or look into online courses, which can range from free courses courtesy of iTunes U to semester-long courses from accredited universities. Some employers may even contribute to course-related expenses. If you have school-age children, can you participate in a parent-teacher organisation? How else could you volunteer while abroad? Teaching English is a popular option.

Build a supportive network abroad

It's important to remain connected to your family and friends back home, but that's not enough. For those living in a city or area with lots of other expats, reach out to other spouses (for the most part wives) who can relate to what you are going through. Meet them, talk to them, find out how they cope with their blues, and use them to help you settle in to your life abroad. For expats who are in more rural or "hardship" locations that lack an extensive expat network, get online. Expat forums such as Expat Women can provide a sense of community.

8.3 Children and other family members

Childcare and schooling

When it comes to your children, their emotional needs will far outweigh practical concerns. However, you shouldn't underestimate the issue of childcare and education. As local day-care facilities in larger towns and major cities often have extremely long waiting lists, it might be wise to register your child in advance before your move back home. This can require a bit of tenacity and persuasion. Many facilities might initially reject or dismiss your application as you aren't a local resident yet. Remember, when it comes to schooling, to choose a system as close to the one that the child may have to return to and try to keep the same philosophy of education alive.

Silvia found it wonderful at first that the school system in England seemed to be a little more relaxed than the one she had got to know in Germany. Brazilian born herself, she found that German schooling was stressful for both parents and children and that there was far too much pressure on children to perform and to bring home good grades. The school at which she had enrolled her two children seemed to have a more balanced approach to learning and it was attractive to Silvia. There was less emphasis on good grades and being the best in class and a far stronger focus on the child's individual best. This was a good start for Silvia who perceived less stress for her children to be less stress for her – at least on one front. What is a very important consideration, though, is that the children will have to return to the German school system where the emphasis on grades will not have disappeared. Silvia needs to strike a balance between what she knows from Germany and what her children will be exposed to in England so that they do not have difficulties on their return. An alternative is to look for a school closer in its education philosophy to the one that her children attend in England when once the family returns to Germany.

Include your children

While you are struggling with your move abroad, try not to forget about your children. It is easy to simply brush their worries aside, but remember that they are often as nervous as you are. After all, they are also in on your move abroad. Set aside some extra time early on to explain to your children why, when and where you are going to move to. They are part of the deal so involve them in the process. Give them little tasks such as helping to pack their belongings in boxes or planning a farewell party with their best friends.

Stay in touch with your family and friends at home

When you move abroad, you will always be leaving someone behind. Thus it is important to find an easy and fun way to keep in touch with your loved ones. Social networks and blogs are good ways to let everyone know you have arrived safely. Once you and your family are settled in, you may want to consider setting up a blog or photo gallery with snapshots from your new home. Sending letters and postcards the old-fashioned way is also a nice way to keep in touch. Children will also enjoy receiving packages and mail from their old home too. It is important to have some sort of regular schedule for keeping in touch, so your friends won't feel neglected. Bear in mind international time differences and set a fixed time and date for phone calls to family and closest friends. These times will not always work, but at least there will be an intended plan in place. Staying in touch with friends and family abroad can give you a sense of security and belonging, particularly at the beginning of your assignment. Needless to say that it is even more important for your children.

CHAPTER 9
NETWORKING FOR NORMALITY

Many expatriates tend to spend most of their time with other expats. Of course, this makes a lot of sense and is an important part of living abroad and finding familiarity soon after your arrival in a new country. As soon as you feel settled, do make a concerted effort to get to know, and blend in with, your host country's culture. The sooner you do this, the sooner you will feel at home.

9.1 Get to know your host culture

When you travel, remember that a foreign country is not designed to make you comfortable. It is designed to make its own people comfortable.

Clifton Fadiman

Before you even start, remember one golden rule: you are a guest in a host culture, so never insult your guests. To know the culture of your host country means to immerse yourself in it. No matter what corner of the earth you end up in, there will be a lot to discover about the history, social customs, national holidays, festivities and traditions of your host country. Some of your non-expat friends may even invite you to a festival or a holiday dinner. This depends on how formal or close personal relationships are in your host culture. It is also a perfect opportunity, of course, to find out how people celebrate in your host country. The casual and relaxed atmosphere of a party among friends will help you to break down the barriers between different nationalities. Initially accept all invitations that you get – this way you can get to know different people and different activities and later on you can choose more specifically who you would like to spend more time with and what kind of activities and interests appeal to you and your family. Also go and say hello – introduce yourself to neighbours or even employees in the local bank or veggie market that you are going to be visiting frequently.

9.2 How much of a new thing is a good thing?

This is up to you and varies from person to person. Influencing factors will be, among other things, upbringing, the culture you have grown up in, your international experience, your personality type – whether you are introverted or rather extroverted by nature.

Many people use the term "going native" to describe moving to a new culture and living and acting exactly as locals do. The idea is that you will endear yourself to the culture faster and be able to adapt more quickly. You adopt everything you can about the new culture: dress, shopping habits, speech, communication style, etc.

The other end of the spectrum is that you change nothing. You celebrate the same holidays in the same ways. You watch the same movies you did back home. You pack your suitcase filled with things from home that you cannot easily find in the new host culture – for me, it was Biltong, a very South African thing (dried meat), or a special South African brand of mayonnaise that I couldn't find anywhere except online at exorbitant prices. My brother in New Zealand was so desperate for some of this classy cream that we sent him a package of it – only to hear of his huge disappointment when it was confiscated and destroyed at customs, which forbids the import of any foodstuffs or related articles that may contain eggs. And so you live and learn and find a local brand that you can deal with or pay five times more for it when you are really desperate – at least until you get back on home soil where you can then overdose on your favourite brand.

In choosing when to completely change and when to remain the same, your host country will be a big determinant in this decision. Is your new home very tight, or very loose? In a tight culture such as Saudi Arabia, keeping your tradition of singing Christmas carols door-to-door might not be a good idea. However, if you are in a loose culture such as Thailand, it is much less likely that anyone will care about your random singing in the streets. Once you know what kind of culture you are living in, the important thing to remember is that you don't make this decision once and then forget about it. The choice of when to change and when not to is often very situational, and there will be times when a decision is better for one person compared to another.

9.3 Mingling with the locals

There are many reasons why you should mingle with the locals. The most important one is that they know all the good places. Locals and long-term expats can show you the most beautiful spots around town. No tourist guide book can ever give you the same inside information on where to buy the freshest food, where to get the cheapest deals or where to sip the best cocktails in town. My husband had been in Beijing for a few years and we had done many things and been to many places, but the really special little hideaways and extra special little shops and restaurants were introduced to us by his local colleagues and good friends.

A very good place to start meeting local people is at work. Don't be shy. Introduce yourself to people and tell them that you are new and very curious about your new home country and its culture. As a temporary guest in a country, one is allowed and forgiven for asking what to locals may seem trivial questions. I remember wanting to know about the origin of some bank holidays that I had never celebrated before. The really funny bit was that local people often didn't know either or had simply not given it any thought until I asked. Talk to people about food and how it is prepared and be adventurous and try new things. Of course, there will be certain things that simply don't appeal to you and that you will not want to try and that's fine. Do remember to be polite though, when local people are enjoying their specialities and refrain from pulling faces or making derogatory comments about what is being eaten and how you would never eat the same. The country and its culture is not about you – it's about that country and its culture. Local people can help you understand this new culture, so network with them as often as you can.

Sports clubs, networking groups for professionals, or arts & crafts classes are great places to meet local people. There are also specialist groups and organisations for expats that have satellite branches in many cities and countries around the world – one such is Internations (www.internations.org). This particular organisation has members who are expats and local members who have been expats somewhere else and are interested in other cultures and international networking. If you have accompanied your spouse abroad and are unable to get a work permit, you can volunteer for a local charity or become involved in a community organisation instead. If you really want to, there is always a way of mingling with the locals.

9.4 Learn the lingo

If you want to make non-expat friends, you need to be ready to speak the local language and get out of your comfort zone. This may seem scary at first, but it will help you to quickly adjust to living abroad. The language barrier is one of those obstacles that are especially hard to overcome when living in another country. The less knowledge you have of the local language prior to your arrival, the longer it will take you to become fluent. However, your language skills will improve swiftly if you use your time abroad to chat with random people such as your neighbour, the mailman or the shop assistant at the corner store. When you understand the language, you get a different insight into the culture. Your efforts to learn the local language will also be appreciated when local people see that you are trying to speak their language. You too will feel an incredible sense of pride and new-found independence as you discover that you can order things, ask for help or explain how you feel in the local language. You know that with a language "if you don't use it, you'll lose it". Don't make that mistake. Start using it and your fluency will improve. And not only will your fluency improve. While living in another country, you will also begin to pick up common expressions and colloquialisms. Maybe you will not use them correctly right away. You may be recognised as a stranger and some of the locals might have a good laugh at you – just remember that it is well-meaning laughter and taking it all with a touch of humour will get you to your goal even more quickly. Try to practise in a secure, non-threatening environment and you will soon get to grips with the local lingo. And when you make mistakes and feel a bit embarrassed, you can always fall back on your "exotic bonus status" of being "new" and still learning.

9.5 You're human – give yourself time

It is tempting to share your experiences of living in a foreign country exclusively with other expats. Nobody else will understand your hesitation to try the local food, your problems with adjusting to the pace of life and your ambivalence towards social customs as well as those who are in the same boat. Many expats who live in another country find comfort in mingling with fellow expats. After all, they share the same experiences, the same problems and the same culture shock. Life abroad can be tough, and sharing your experience with someone who understands it immediately can have a very comforting effect. Do this when you feel the need to. Don't put pressure on yourself to "go totally native". You know yourself best and some people take comfort from being surrounded by people and traditions they are familiar with, so feel free to do that if you want to. No matter how much you immerse yourself into the new culture, always remain true to those parts of your own culture which inspire you. The wonderful thing about being an expat is that you can mingle with the host culture and experience how the locals live, but when you go home and are within your own four walls, you can be whatever and whoever you want to be. If you like eating spaghetti bolognaise with sugar in it, sprinkle it freely on your portion and enjoy! Listen to the music you want to hear and speak your native tongue with all the slang you can think of.

Many expats have told me that even though they are very happy in their host cultures and partake in many local traditions, they sense a friendly, harmless sense of rebellion when they go to their own home and are often quite silly about "just being me".

Make mistakes and laugh and learn from them

I remember my first Christmas in Bavaria. Having come from South Africa where we celebrate a summer Christmas, I was already quite fascinated by the whole run-up to Christmas that started in the Advent weeks. The wonderful-smelling, quaint Christmas markets were mind-boggling. I loved the wintery atmosphere and couldn't wait to get home at night and light candles and extend the atmosphere at home that I was experiencing on the streets. It felt wonderful and I even started drinking Glühwein (mulled red wine) – a previously unthinkable thought for my Cape Town, wine-region palate. Shortly before the first Advent weekend, my lovely new neighbour wanted to surprise me with a Christmas wreath. I was overwhelmed when I found it at the front door. I rushed over to thank her but she wasn't home and so I went home and in my enthusiasm and excitement prepared a lovely dinner for my husband and I. Central to the atmosphere was the beautiful wreath and its four big candles. I lit them all and looked in awe at how romantic it all seemed. When my unsuspecting husband returned home, he was surprised – in more ways than one. Of course I didn't realise that only one candle gets lit on each Advent Sunday preceding Christmas. We had a good laugh and it is an experience that I still think of fondly today. So make mistakes, laugh and learn from them and enjoy the little surprises that life in a new culture may bestow on you from time to time.

9.6 Cultivating friendships

True friends are not the people that have been in my life the longest – they are those that I know are there when I need them. Friends don't send you on a guilt trip because you are very busy and haven't got round to talking to them or seeing them as much as usual. And there are friends everywhere. Seek and you shall find them. Treasure them and they will accompany you for a lifetime, no matter where your life's journey takes you. True friendships are worth a million but keeping them up as an expat is a challenge. That is why friendships that stand the test of time are so valuable. Here are some ways for making and keeping friendships across continents and time zones:

- Remove the pressure. Good friends lift you up and support you. But at the same time, they don't put pressure on the friendship to be all things to them, at all stages of their lives. They are comfortable with where the friendship is at and they recognise that even the best friendship cannot fulfil all their needs.

- Be adaptable. People change. People move. People grow, and sometimes they grow old. We are each on our own journey and that's OK. People with longstanding friendships are flexible and forgiving. They realise that no person or friendship is perfect. Celebrate each other as you are now, while also sharing the past together.

- Remember special occasions – there is nothing quite as heartwarming as getting a birthday wish or congratulations on an achievement from a friend on foreign shores.

- Time is relevant. Yes, you will have to deal with time differences and friends may be sleeping while you want to chat. Sometimes you have to accept that you won't be able to talk for a while, but really good friends will be there if you are in need – whether it's at ten in the morning or at midnight.

- Exchange information online and share experiences on platforms such as Facebook and WhatsApp. Use Skype calls and videos for a more interactive, personal experience.

- Appreciate the value of a lifelong bond. Lifelong friendships are rare and precious. If you find such friendships cherish them. Because these types of bonds are difficult to forge, these friendships are worth investing in.

CHAPTER 10
THE EXPAT CAREER IN BRIEF

What I would like to share here would be the content for another book – perhaps my next one. I do feel though that no guide for expats would be complete without some mention of the expat career, so I am touching on it briefly with a few thoughts in this chapter. I have worked with many people over many years just before they set off on, and when they return from, expat assignments and I can sum up almost simplistically the main thoughts that they share about the expat and the workplace. In a nutshell then:

- It's never quite as you expect it to be

- Companies are not the same around the world just because they share the same name

- International teams can be strenuous and tiresome

- Companies don't invest enough in international communication culture training

- It's a valuable experience working abroad and you will refer to this time and the experiences regularly for the rest of your working career

- The first time is the toughest – after one assignment, a second one is easier to handle

- Titles and perceptions of power differ radically from country to country

- It's usually a rewarding and enriching experience for both the expat and their family – on a personal and financial level

10.1 The Lewis model of management culture

In his world-famous book *When Cultures Collide*[3], Richard D. Lewis looks at the phenomenon of how to manage successfully across cultures. In this astoundingly insightful book, he explains how managers can be successful regardless of which culture they work in. Before embarking on your stint as an international leader, make sure that you find out as much as you can about the host culture you are going to be leading and leading in. Speak to other business leaders from the same culture and get as much information as you can to ease your start as a manager in a foreign country.

Demonstrating leadership competency across cultural boundaries is no easy task. Hundreds and often times thousands of years of cultural nuances have impacted the way each civilisation operates. Nuggets of wisdom, passed from generation to generation come together to form the slowly evolving backbone of a society. As a leader, you certainly do not want to clash against a deeply entrenched

---

3 *When Cultures Collide: Managing Successfully Across Cultures.* London: Nicholas Brealey Publishing, 1996.

culture. In order to succeed, leaders must understand and embrace the culture of the people they intend to lead. This begs the question, "how do you know what leadership style is best for a specific culture?" In the early 1990s, British linguist and cross-cultural communications expert Richard Lewis developed a model that helps to shed some light on the way that different cultures communicate. It provides a great, generalised definition that leaders can use to adjust their leadership style to meet the cultural needs of their people.

In the model, Lewis draws a triangle between three distinct ways of interacting:

- Linear active – task-oriented and very organised planners who are data-oriented

- Multi-active – people-oriented and talkative interactors who are dialogue-oriented

- Reactive – introverted and respectful listeners who are listening-oriented

- In between each of these three points are degrees of difference that make up a continuum of cultures. Lewis maps different cultures along these lines to provide an easy way to understand the cultural nuances of a particular country. When looking at his model of cultural types keep in mind that these are generalisations that can be made about a specific culture. Remember this caveat: individual sub-groups within the culture or even differences from team to team will exist. The model is simply the backdrop behind which individuals operate.

10.2 Gamification

Though the term "gamification" was coined in 2002 by Nick Pelling, a British-born computer programmer and inventor, it did not gain popularity until 2010. As a leader or a team player and even as an individual worker, it would be good to have an idea of what types of players make up the workplace. Corporations are made by people and hence, to a large extent, the corporate reality is shaped and dependent on employees' personal involvement and individual values systems. There are many professionally and privately fulfilled managers and there are also those who complain about being unhappy and burned out. To be perfectly fair, each corporation is different and represents different cultures and work styles that might or might not be suitable for everyone. However it is worth remembering that in each group there are rules which allow you to fit into the existing reality. It is important to be aware of who you are and what your role in the corporation is. "Gamification" is the term describing the use of game mechanics and dynamics to increase the personal involvement in areas that are not directly related to the world of games.

There are four types of players distinguished in this theory:

1. The killers

They are focused on fight and risk. They derive satisfaction from overcoming others. They are usually pragmatic, efficient, goal-oriented and not afraid of confrontations. They are perfect for positions where aggressive and decisive actions are desirable.

2. Achievers

They are focused on challenges and development. Achievers are motivated by results. They like working in a group. They do not need a large degree of control and they work best with limited supervision. There is a danger when a company is not able to motivate them with the next big challenge as they tend to get bored. Another threat is the direct confrontation with the killers. Achievers do not want to waste time on confrontations. Killers are ruled by the need to compete where achievers are ruled by ambition so the definition of "win" is very different.

3. Socialites

They want everybody to be fine! They derive the energy from their work relationship. They build a network of contacts to support their ideas. Usually they work in HR, PR and wherever the road is what counts and not the end result.

4. Explorers

They derive energy from solving problems. They are not always interested in the effect or purpose. They delve into the analysis and might sometimes lose focus of the actual goal.

Typically we combine characteristics from each player but usually there is one that dominates. It is worth emphasising that it is important to play the game that is based on your own system of values!

So what are the rules in a corporate game?

1. Stay in the profit zone

It is not the statement of the year that corporations work for profit. Staying in the profit zone seems to be the simplest to describe in sales and marketing, but in difficult times it is also associated with the risk of defeat and lack of results. However, not everyone has to be the leader going up the corporate ladder. One can be fulfilled working in a specialist position as not everybody wants or is expected to have a dynamic career and spectacular effects at work. Sometimes simply performing your task well does the trick.

2. Set your goals well

Don't think that others will take care of you. Set the objectives and tasks by yourself. Do what you are being paid for and what you are expected to be doing, focusing on the tasks and results your performance evaluation is based on. Remember your responsibilities and learn how to say "no" to others. Of course it does not mean that you do not have to engage in other projects, especially the interesting ones, but make sure that your duties do not suffer because of this.

3. Build relationships with the right people

This is the basis of survival and development in large organisations. Take care of your relationships with people, thanks to which you can achieve your business goals easier. Teamwork and communication are two of the most valued skills in corporations.

4. Do not overshadow your boss

A big chunk of your career in a corporation depends on your boss and the relationship between the two of you. Do not allow any situation in which you appear smarter or more important. Competition between you and your boss will probably end badly for you – regardless of whether you are actually better than them.

5. Take care of yourself

Learn to promote yourself well. The results of your hard work should be known to your boss and if possible to the boss of your boss as well.

The key to happiness in a corporation is to create a distance between work and yourself. A distanced and flexible work style together with conscious commitment will allow you to feel and function better. Rather than getting frustrated by negative thoughts and emotions, learn how to play.

10.3 Inside international business culture

Knowing and understanding the unwritten rules of international business culture is important, whether you're on a business trip or working abroad as an expat. Business etiquette is a vast subject which inevitably varies from country to country. In fact, the term "international business culture" might seem misleading, as there is hardly "one" single, monolithic approach. So while the term does not refer to one specific culture, it raises people's awareness of the fact that business happens in an international and cross-cultural context. Doing business abroad requires an understanding of this international context – a certain degree of cultural awareness.

Knowing how foreign cultures differ from your own and what kind of behaviour you should expect and avoid is probably the first step in the right direction. It is essential that you leave an "our way is the best way" attitude at home and try to adjust to a different world. Your business partners know that many unwritten rules are new to you and will surely forgive you some minor etiquette mistakes. However, if your overall attitude is the problem, you will probably watch quite a few business relationships go sour. I remember so well Alf H., a successful Herman top manager on his way to lead a team of line managers in England. I was most concerned as we spoke about ways of leading people and he said things such as, "I am not going there to win a popularity contest. I know the business and they will soon learn that it's my way or no way." Absolutely resistant to any kind of suggestions from anybody else, he set off with his management style tightly tucked in his pocket. Three months later, he was back in Germany. The assignment had been terminated by his German boss in the UK on the basis that he lacked all feeling for working internationally and had close to zero social competence in the work place.

Fortunately, there are countless books on international business culture and even a number of smartphone applications which allow you to quickly look up the most important advice on national and international business culture.

Gift-giving

Gift-giving is probably one of the trickiest aspects of international business culture. In some countries, presenting small gifts early on in a business relationship is expected. In others, it may be perceived as a bribe and will therefore be an offence to your business partners. And then there are those special cases in which gifts are expected at a later point, after a solid business relationship has been established.

The rules of receiving and treating gifts also vary greatly within international business culture. In Asia and the Middle East, gifts, much like business cards, are received with either both hands or your right hand, respectively. In Singapore or China, the recipient may politely decline the gift three times before accepting it. While it is considered extremely rude in many Asian countries to open a gift in the presence of the gift-giver, people from many South American countries, such as Chile, tend to open gifts right away.

When choosing a gift, try to keep the religious and social context of your host country in mind. A bottle of good wine or champagne may be an acceptable token at home. In Muslim countries, however, it can be a violation of religious laws and an offence to your business partners. The same is true for certain types of food, such as pork in predominantly Muslim or Jewish countries, or beef in countries with a big Hindu population, such as India. Aside from religious laws, there are other pitfalls when it comes to gift-giving. Certain objects and colour schemes can have a negative meaning and should be avoided. In China, clocks and watches are considered unlucky too, so the Swiss CEO would do well not to try and impress the Chinese CEO with a good watch from Switzerland. Choose something red instead – this colour represents good luck. Whatever type of gift you choose in the end, make sure that it has some value. Avoid gifts that bear your company's logo. Business dinners are often treated as gifts. If you receive an invitation, you should definitely reciprocate. Not only will it show your appreciation of your business contacts, but also present you as an accomplished person versed in the rules of international business culture. Clearly, different companies have different rules depending on their compliance policies, so be sure to find out what the relevant one for you is.

CHAPTER 11
GOING HOME AND THE REPATRIATION PROCESS

You went through the expat preparation phase before you left home, so not all of this is new. You're just preparing to go back home, which, on the face of it, should be simpler than it was leaving home. A common problem here is that the return dates often come far faster than expats can imagine. Settled in and getting on with life in the countries of their choice, expats are often not prepared for actually packing up and moving out.

11.1 Planning repatriation

Your move back home after spending quite some time abroad can be a stressful experience for all parties. There are times when it will feel as if you have really returned to the drawing board you were sitting at before you left home. Sorting out the paperwork and taking care of other matters can make repatriation an unpleasant task.

Many repatriates are not as well supported in the process of getting back home as they are in the process of getting away from home. There is often the false assumption made by **HR** departments of companies, but also by the expats themselves, that returning home should be a walk in the park – after all, it's familiar territory and the expat knows where he's going back to.

Give yourself sufficient time to plan your repatriation. Draw up to-do lists and don't leave everything till the last month. This will go a long way to making your return less stressful.

Paperwork

Contact your nearest embassy or consulate to find out whether any specific re-entry regulations might affect your return. For example, if there are certain health risks in the country where you have been recently living, you might be required to get a medical certificate or even spend some time in quarantine. Moreover, you should make sure that your passport or other travel documents are valid. If there have been any changes in your family status during your time as an expatriate, e.g. if you had a child on foreign soil or if you were divorced, you need to inform your embassy of this as well. You will also have to cancel rental agreements, utilities – including internet and phone provision – and settle any outstanding bills. Furthermore, if there is compulsory registration in your host country, don't forget to officially inform the local authorities of when you will be leaving.

Forward mail

Make sure to enquire at the local post office whether it's possible to forward your mail to your home in another country. If such a service is not available, try asking local friends whether they are willing to receive and send you any important mail that arrives after your departure. Also make sure to cancel any regular deliveries or subscriptions you might have.

Finance and insurance

In addition to paperwork, your finances are another important item that need to be sorted out. Consider how monetary issues might affect your move: How expensive will your new city of residence be? Can you afford the average cost of living with your current family income when your expat allowance is gone? Will your impending move cut into your savings? Now is the right moment to get in touch with your financial adviser and ask how to time your move for tax minimisation. This is also the perfect opportunity to get further information on benefits, pensions, and insurance in your home country and on whether any social security contributions you've paid abroad are transferable.

And last but not least, make sure that there is an easy option for paying outstanding bills from abroad if you can't settle them all before you leave.

11.2 Getting back to normal

Returning home can be very stressful for all family members – children have to get to know their friends again or meet completely new ones. Adults have to reconnect with friends and family members who may have no idea what being an expat means and may not be able to share enthusiasm about the expat experience or even have sympathy with the tough times you may have had abroad. In the first few weeks, friends, and relatives at home will mostly be supportive and happy that you are back, but this may change. Unless they have been expats themselves, they will neither know nor understand what it means to be an "invisible immigrant" and how to best support former expats in their coming home from an international assignment.

Anke, 54 years old, resigned from her job to join her husband for three years in South Africa. She loved the country, its people and all it had to offer and was happy to have left behind her what she referred to as "the little grey, foggy village with nothing to offer". She soaked up the African sun and took up many new hobbies. Within a very short time, Anke had a diary fuller than when she was working full-time and a list of new friends and acquaintances that kept her busy most of the time. She enjoyed horse riding, something she had always dreamed of when she was back home, but never got round to because, in her words, "it was too expensive and the weather was always horrible". It was the same with golf. Anke took up the sport and after several lessons and practice, spent at least one day a week on the golf course. Her perception of her expat home was that it was far superior to the one she had left behind.

On her return, Anke found it very difficult resettling in the village she had left behind three years earlier. She was soon depressed and dreamed of her time in Africa. She felt that everybody around her had changed and that people were not the same as before. She felt that even her closest friends and family members were envious as opposed to enthusiastic and excited as she relayed her stories from South Africa. She clashed with them more and more as they got tired about hearing how "things were far better there". Of course what had happened, was that

Anke had changed. Her experiences abroad had started to become normal for her and she took her new way of life for granted – forgetting of course that she would return to the country of her departure and that it would have remained largely unchanged.

Readjustment issues

Some former expatriates like Anke do indeed feel an acute loss in status and significance throughout their repatriation process. In her expat country where the cost of living was far lower than she had been used to, she lived a life of leisure and luxury and benefitted from the many perks her husband's company offered their expats. Returning to her more mundane sort of life back home was very difficult and depressing for Anke and it was only with therapy that she managed to settle down again and enjoy life back home. Anke keeps in touch with friends abroad, but has also joined a group of former-expat partners and they regularly meet for lively exchanges of their times abroad in a forum where people know what it means to be both an ex- and a repatriate.

Three years, or any amount of time abroad for that matter, will change you. It will help you learn, grow, and develop. It will open your eyes to a new culture, to a different climate, and to a whole new world of food, not to mention a different outlook on life. While repatriation comes sooner or later, the expat experiences you have abroad will last for life.

11.3 The repatriate and the work place

Many expats are so excited at the prospect of leaving for a new country and a new assignment with all it has to offer, that they completely lose sight of where they are leaving from and, more importantly, of where they will ultimately come back to. It is important to remember that most expats do come back home and that the less contact they have with home while they're away, the less home will think about or remember them on their return. Often, expat contracts include lucrative accommodation or transport packages, which enable expats to drive expensive cars and live in above-average accommodation. After being used to such standards, it can be difficult to cope with the loss of these special perks when you come back home.

11.4 Prepare for repatriation when you're planning to leave home

Nowadays, it is a great risk to move abroad on an expat assignment. Many companies do not support their employees well upon return or struggle to create a suitable job opening for them. Therefore, expats should find out how supportive their company is before they actually go abroad. Expats-to-be should find out if their company is well prepared to send them abroad. Colleagues who have already gone through the process should be the first ones you talk to. They can offer inside information on how well a company supports their expats. Also ensure that a repatriation agreement is laid down in the contract before the assignment even begins. This should include an agreement on your position after repatriation (one equal to or better than what you held before the assignment) as well as an answer regarding the issue of who is covering the various costs connected with repatriation, such as the shipment of goods.

Many expats leave with additional baggage and are given generous air freight allowances to get their most important belongings abroad. All too often, such expats return with many more belongings, including furniture and other bulky items acquired abroad. This is when air freight becomes too costly and container transport is required. With the help of such a repatriation agreement you can avoid landing in an unsuitable or unwanted position when returning home. Often expats need to remind their employers that a suitable position upon return will benefit the company because of the expat's new-found international experience and bigger-picture view of the organisation that they had previously left. Negotiate with your employer for a better position and state positively what your experience can add to the company's success. Sell your abilities and career development in the right way, especially if you have acquired some special knowledge – perhaps not just insider expertise about the country you have come from, but also a command of the language spoken there. Use network partners to help set yourself up for a good job on your return, whether that is with the one you started out from or with a completely new one that may just be looking for exactly the kind of experience you have brought back home.

AUTHOR BIO

Marinda Seisenberger is an expert on ***international communication culture***. The native South African of Irish/Dutch descent has headed three different, profit-based institutes for adult education in South Africa and led the corporate communications division of an Egyptian-led African Development company in the same country. Both career and private pursuits have taken her around the globe to finally settle in Bavaria, Germany, where she lives to this day. From 1999 to 2014, she built up and owned a language and intercultural skills training company in Germany. Today, as a trainer, speaker and coach, Seisenberger supports and advises her customers on how best to live and work internationally. An expat herself and the wife of an expat, Seisenberger has lived and worked in different parts of South Africa, in Egypt, Mozambique, Namibia, England and Germany. With direct family members located in South Africa, New Zealand, Ireland, China and Dubai, internationality and expatriate experience is a central part of her life – an interesting, multi-faceted and ever-evolving part.

Lightning Source UK Ltd.
Milton Keynes UK
UKOW05f0957030615

252805UK00002B/6/P